D0939007

FETISHISM AND IMAGINATION

David Simpson teaches in the Department of English at North-western University. He is the author of *Wordsworth and the Figurings of the Real* and of *Irony and Authority in Romantic Poetry*.

FETISHISM
and IMAGINATION
Dickens, Melville, Conrad

David Simpson

THE JOHNS HOPKINS UNIVERSITY PRESS
BALTIMORE AND LONDON

The Johns Hopkins University Press, Baltimore, Maryland 21218
The Johns Hopkins Press Ltd., London

Library of Congress Cataloging in Publication Data

Simpson, David, 1951–
    Fetishism and imagination.

    Bibliography: pp. 133–37
    Includes index.
    1. English fiction—History and criticism.   2. Fetishism in
literature.   3. Dickens, Charles, 1812–1870—Criticism and interpretation.   4. Melville, Herman, 1819–1891—Criticism and
interpretation.   5. Conrad, Joseph, 1857–1924—Criticism and
interpretation.   I. Title.
PR 830.F48S5   823′.009   82–238
ISBN 0-8018-2858-9   AACR2

For my friends and colleagues
at King's College, Cambridge

*In a word, Frederick Cuvier's Sperm Whale is not a Sperm Whale, but a squash. . . .
Though elephants have stood for their full-lengths, the living Leviathan has never yet fairly
floated himself for his portrait. The living whale, in his full majesty and significance, is only
to be seen at sea in unfathomable waters; and afloat the vast bulk of him is out of sight, like
a launched line-of-battle ship; and out of that element it is a thing eternally impossible for
mortal man to hoist him bodily into the air, so as to preserve all his mighty swells and
undulations.*

Melville, *Moby-Dick*

CONTENTS

PREFACE

In the passage I have chosen as the epigraph to this book, Ishmael dismisses Cuvier's attempt at rendering the image of the sperm whale by invoking the authority of first-hand observation. But it is, peculiarly, the authority of nonobservation, of an empirically discovered blindness or futility. As so often in *Moby-Dick*, Ishmael is telling us what the whale is not rather than what it is. It may indeed by *like* a whole series of things, among them a line-of-battle ship, in certain of its particular attributes, and the novel is profusely supplied with such analogies. But as a living whole the whale cannot be imaged. Even direct experience, he later tells us, provides only a "tolerable idea" of the whale's identity; and this, given the risks involved, might be better avoided.

Moby-Dick, glimpsed briefly as he is throughout the voyage but so often transmitted to us in the language of negation or nondefinition, may be thought of as refusing—even as he attracts—the fetishistic energies that some of his pursuers, and Ahab most especially, seek to focus upon him. Ishmael himself, as observer and participant, seems divided, and his language may suggest the motives behind his ambivalence. Even as the impossibility of the whale ever being turned successfully into graven image or rigid form is being asserted, antithetical currents seem to flow within the narration. *Mortal* man cannot hoist the whale out of the ocean for complete inspection, but perhaps man could become more than mortal? . . . For most of us, "full majesty" is *seen* only in "unfathomable waters": fullness must then consist in some degree of concealment. Does Ahab tease Ishmael with the prospect that this need not be so, convincing him of the nobility of what must be judged to be a death wish even as he outrages his reflective moral intelligence?

For it is only death which can provide Ahab with the completion that he compulsively seeks. The white whale is life-in-death, death-dealing as his briefly apprehended majesty is suggestive of infinite life. And death invades the very language and aspiration of definition. One can kill other whales, of course, and hoist them out of the water, but they are then no longer images of the living: they do not represent the truth Ishmael here ponders. Visible dead image, or mysterious living organism: there seems to be nothing between. What is there in the context of Ishmael's meditations that might help to explain this seemingly irreducible fusion of life and death—life imaged in death—and the urgency to represent what can only be represented by the supersession of all that is most true to life? Why is communication, between characters in novels as between narrators and their readers, thus bedevilled by the deadness of images?

What follows is the second half of an inquiry into the ethics of perception and representation as evidenced in certain important nineteenth-century writers. The first part of this inquiry dealt with Wordsworth, and has been published as *Wordsworth and the Figurings of the Real* (London: Macmillan, 1982). The subject matter of the present book, though related to that of its predecessor, has been rendered self-explanatory. Nevertheless, a few summary comments are here in place, to indicate the emphases and conclusions of my reading of Wordsworth and of the Romantic priority he represents. They will explain why Wordsworth is at times invoked herein as the proponent of an increasingly threatened ideal.

That he was the proponent of an ideal did not of course make him merely its uncomplicated observer. For the ideal of polymorphous perception in Wordsworth's writing, whereby the flexible mind discovers its most creative identity in the incoherent elements of experience and the dizzying fluctuations between extremes—joy and sorrow, fear and beauty, rain and sun—is already framed within a sense of its recent or imminent disappearance. The marginal society of owner-occupiers inhabiting the remoter parts of the Lake District, places thinly populated by both people and natural objects (a few trees, a few mountains, a few sheep), is presented by Wordsworth as the last remaining model of an environment in which the human imagination can most healthily function.

That this model is presented within a mythology of loss does open the question of Wordsworth's intentions and effects as a 'radical' writer. However we resolve it, it is at least clear that it is no mere sentimental attraction for the rustic life which informs the urgency of his dissent from what he saw as a dangerous historical trend. On the contrary, Wordsworth's writings contain a fully worked-out theory of the human mind as it is open to various forms of social construction. For him, all perception is selective and figurative, constructing a 'reality' out of a complex interaction between sense data, the mechanics of the brain, and social and individual idiosyncrasies. Of these three elements composing perception it is the last which is most variable, most open to control, and consequently most urgently debated in accounting for the ways in which people fail to share a common reality. To a degree that I shall not try to recapitulate here, Wordsworth's poems and critical writings constitute a detailed account of the ways in which, particularly, people in cities will 'see' a different world from that seen by people in the country. The city person sees graven images, theatrical representations, and superficially gratifying figures, driven to them as he is by the monotony of his daily habits and occupations which make him unable to exercise a creative intelligence upon the forms put before his eyes. The country person, on the other hand, is less afflicted by a division between work and leisure, less pressured by an extreme of subservience to require compensation in a contrary extreme of mastery. The country person has a less fixed image of reality. He is kept on his toes by being exposed to all the vicissitudes of an uncontrollable nature, and by being less exposed to an environment dominated by ready-made signs calling for passive acceptance rather than active recreation.

This difference between the two realities perceived by the two classes of person meant that, in any arguments or divisions of interest between their respective societies, victory would always go to the stronger, since the dominance of their very construction of reality would effectively prevent them even perceiving, let alone considering, the claims of alternatives. In this way Wordsworth saw the city to be destroying the country, not simply by conscious aggression but by redetermining its very image in the minds of the majority of men.

Only in ideal environments could the human mind expect to preserve (or develop) a healthful and regenerative mode of perception. Otherwise it must lapse (or develop) into passivity and torpor, seeing a world of dead relations rather than living images. One of the most common ways in which the Romantics and their successors described this problem was by invoking the vocabulary of fetishism. Roughly speaking, fetishism occurs when the mind ceases to realize that it has itself created the outward images or things to which it subsequently posits itself as in some sort of subservient relation. Fear of this tendency in the mind, which always needs *some* element of outward form if it is to function at all, informs Romantic ethics and aesthetics at all levels. Coleridge's idea of the "symbol," to give but one example (one I mention below as a frequent point of contrast), is designed to try to preempt the separation of part from whole, letter from spirit, vehicle of meaning from *act* of *making* meaning itself. The symbol is "an actual and essential part of that, the whole of which it represents." It is "not a metaphor or allegory or any other figure of speech or form of fancy," but "a living part in that Unity, of which it is the representative."[1] Such emphasis on the living process means that any contemplation of the symbol should also involve awareness and experience of *self*-consciousness. Coleridge's use of this model as an ideal occurrence in all modes of communication, from the perceptual to the political, means that fetishism, or concentration upon the *mere* image, is as far as possible discouraged.

My account of Dickens, Melville, and Conrad will concentrate upon all the factors in their analysis of representation which inhibit any potential dominance of the "symbolic" in the societies they describe. In this way, they are analysts of fetishism. In describing this situation, I have taken over one or two elements of the vocabulary of my earlier book. In particular, the word *figuring* remains appropriate because the implicit epistemology active in the novels discussed is the same as that dramatized by Wordsworth. All 'reality' is recognized as constructed by somebody, though not all perceivers are encouraged to understand this fact. It is thus recognized as a *figure*, a partial and selected model whose very intelligibility depends upon the exclusion of alternative figures. We communicate with ourselves and with others by what Coleridge called "companionable form,"[2] modes of relation which we select or have imposed upon us.

The book begins with an introductory account of the place of fetishism in the theological, moral, and aesthetic arguments current in the eighteenth and nineteenth centuries. In the context of a traditional Puritan suspicion of the worship of outward forms, I try here to construct a historical, discursive context for the particular priorities examined in the three novelists. Dickens is then presented as a critic of the fetishized imagination, as it results in a topsy-turvy world wherein all authentic relations are inverted or excluded. This world is an energetic mechanism, the perpetual friction between the uncoordinated parts never creating anything whole.

In the generally fetishized world Dickens presents, one in which various idols are worshipped and various body parts or attributes made the focus of exclusive attention, I trace hints of an awareness of the phallicism which had already been seen by earlier commentators to be at the heart of the syndrome of fetishism. This theme is further developed in a reading of *Moby-Dick*. Something of the same energy of misattribution and disjunction appearing in Dickens is also analysed by Melville. Whatever negative results may accrue from the pursuit of the *grandissimus*, located as it is as the ungraspable focus of man's physical and metaphysical imagination, there is yet a complexity of negative and positive in Ishmael's reporting of the chasing of the whale. In part, this may be due to the fact that Moby-Dick survives. He stands for a nature that, as ideally in Wordsworth, is uncontrollable and beyond man's capacity to deaden it.

What is in *Moby-Dick* a crescendo of moral ambiguity is but faintly echoed in Conrad. His novels reproduce a world in which all heroic energies seem to be dying for want of air, as they elide all the functions that in earlier writings had operated as bearers of light; women and children become scarce and insignificant, as experiences of creative heterogeneity in the environment at large also disappear. There are no depths to the sea, no grand quests for completion, and no pervasively effective counterforces in nature to stimulate the human mind into modesty. Typhoons and high seas may indeed chasten some, but the successful are blessed by a blunt perseverance, even an ignorance, which carries them through. Heroic as they may in a strange sense thus appear, their lack of endangering imagination also threatens to make them little more than efficient company servants, and the companies do not, as we shall see, come in for much in the way of approval. Those gifted with a sense of alternatives, on the other hand, seem to undo themselves. The man of action and the man of imagination are really just two elements in a uniformly miscreating world, whatever preferences we may have between them.

Melville and (particularly) Conrad demonstrate the exporting of the fetishized imagination from one's own society to distant places; the very places from which, ironically enough, the first accounts of fetishistic practices had originally been taken. I include some remarks on the history of fetishism as an anthropological concept, and on the way in which such specific formulations relate to its incidence in the novels discussed. Having originated as a way of describing pagan practices, *fetishism* comes to apply far more thoroughly and dangerously to social developments in the 'civilized' world. The writers I discuss are important if implicit commentators on the ongoing process of inversion between the primitive and the civilized, a process that Rousseau had focused if not set in motion. At the end of the cycle, in Conrad, the primitive no longer has an identity of its own. It has been almost completely repossessed, and of course represented, by a colonial consciousness that is far more completely fetishized and far more efficiently monolithic than anything in the undeveloped world.

Like all arguments that are sustained through a range of writers and over a considerable period of history, what follows has obvious shortcomings, prescribed indeed in the very nature of its ambitions. My interest is in the changing ideas about the nature and consequences of selectivity in representation, and I have of course myself been selective. There is no attempt here at a complete reading of any of the authors. This reservation applies most of all to Melville, whose integrity as an American writer especially, as well as as the author of major novels besides *Moby-Dick*, is somewhat ignored. There were, of course, aspects of his tradition which could be used to locate him firmly within the spectrum of ideas I am discussing. European Romanticism came to America as an influential force, and it came up against an important Puritan tradition. The confluence of these two streams offers one way of estimating the American identity of Melville,[3] and it will be clear that such a confluence both relates to and differs from the situation in nineteenth-century England. I have not tried to situate Melville in these terms. Nor have I attempted the kind of book that Ian Watt, for example, implicitly commends in the following remarks from his *Conrad in the Nineteenth Century*:

> There are many reasons why the literary critic tends to be suspicious of the history-of-ideas approach . . . in general the search for such portable intellectual contents as can conveniently be pried loose from a literary work deflects attention from what it can most genuinely yield, and at best gives in return a few abstract ideas whose nature and interrelationships are much more exactly stated in formal philosophy. In any case the greatest authors are rarely representative of the ideology of their period; they tend rather to expose its internal contradic-

tions or the very partial nature of its capacity for dealing with the facts of experience. This seems to be true of Shakespeare; it seems to be even truer as we approach the modern world, where no single intellectual system has commanded anything like general acceptance.[4]

Without trying to pass any kind of measured judgment on Watt's book, I should like to use this passage as an exemplary statement of the values and assumptions directed by many literary critics against the sort of book that follows this preface. The antithesis between 'prying loose' and 'yielding' tells all. The one approach partakes of architectural vandalism, bearing away illegal souvenirs that show no relation to the whole fabric of the building when seen in isolation and made exemplary. They are the products of disrespect and blindness. The other, favored, approach subsists by sympathetic cooperation, offering no violence and thus allowing the spontaneously expressive functions of the edifice to appear. They "yield" to the tact of the interpreter, who is thus the true literary critic.

What I should most like to question is whether great authors really are "rarely representative of the ideology of their period." An answer depends, of course, on what one chooses to make of "ideology" and of the similarly scorned "history of ideas." If we think of them as simple models of experience which the writer is meant to reflect in a simple and uncomplicated way, then it would be hard not to confirm Watt's right to dismiss. I suppose that every exponent of every academic discipline tends by profession of faith to believe in the superior accuracy of his own method, and it has been said of literary critics, not entirely without justification, that we are the more anxious and assertive about our position because of the frailty of our forms of consensus and the uneasiness of our eclecticism. But it is not necessary, unless we are for some reason committed in an a priori way to reductive thinking, to think of "ideology" as a discursive superfluity that runs alongside literature but in a different and shallower channel, offering to the researcher only the most superficial parallels that the inspection of literature itself always renders more complicated. To rob ideas and ideology of complexity and contradiction is to impoverish them and to establish a false dichotomy between literature and other forms of expression and analysis. Nor, I think, can we continue to get away with an assumption about the privileged access of literature to the "facts of experience." I would doubt whether any form of reflective writing, and perhaps any writing at all, could afford such access, even if it does employ the language of 'life as it is lived.' Once we recognize that experience takes place at least partly and perhaps largely in the mind, and that the mind is open to various structurings and motivations, then the language of empirical verification can no longer be taken at face value. Indeed, there is no better example than Melville's *Typee* to remind us of this. Narrated as this book is in the language of first-person experience, we now know that much of what it incorporates was adapted from travel books and literary sources. This need not of course make it any less true to 'experience'; the point is rather that experience itself is a function of a way of being in the world which is different at different times and for different people, and which may be in part composed according to preestablished principles and preoccupations.[5]

This puts literature and the experience it describes or purports to describe right back into play with all the other forms of perception and description which surround it and give it a context, and it explains why this book of mine remains dominantly and deliberately literary critical, referring closely to exemplary works of literature. For, once literary criticism has ceased to wag its finger at other disciplines from atop its unsteady and even imaginary pinnacle as the central humanity, then it can recognize ideas and ideology as complex and sensitive paradigms around and within which the priorities of a particular generation can be seen to be organized. Once we abjure easy reference to the "facts of experience," then such ideas are especially useful for the way in which they suggest that different generations have fashioned different versions of the human and correspondingly different experiences. Thus I hope that readers will not find that fetishism is an extraneous paradigm which dislocates the depths and complexities of the various works of literature to which it is related, but rather a living part of whatever wholes those works might be thought to compose. As such, it speaks for an important element in the moral imperative of literature, and the fact that similar imperatives may be traced in preceding and contemporary writings of different genres makes that literature a living part of history, and in the fullest sense.

This emphasis on historical continuity obliges me to anticipate a likely question. Fetishism is a concept which began by relating to what we now call anthropology, extended into theology and political economy, and ended up rather famously in psychoanalysis and in the theory of sexuality. I use the term in a sense broad enough to risk offending specialists in every one of these disciplines, even as I try to acknowledge their special definitions along the way. What, then, am I implying about the relation of literature to all of these disciplines? Simply that they share a history, the elucidation of which can be mutually informative among them all.

There is one problem that this approach avoids, and another that it creates. That which it avoids would follow the selection of a model from a more recently constituted discipline or theory which is then applied to literature in the past. We take, say, an essay by Lévi-Strauss on a 'primitive' society and use it to come to a reading of, say, a Shakespeare play. In so doing we create a problem by our movement outside history and outside obvious cultural continuity. Such tactics can and do illuminate our readings of literature, and at the very least they create useful classroom controversies. The questions they give rise to are often questions about universals—how it can be that the one seems to fit the other across time and cultural space—though of course they can also be answered by reference to the synthesizing function of our own time and space as it organizes the past (consciously or otherwise) within the framework of its own immediate and contemporary ways of seeing. In the latter case, hermeneutic inquiry replaces or supplements the concern with universals.

These are the questions that my approach avoids. Neither Freud, nor Frazer, nor anyone else is 'read back' to an anterior literature. Of course, any claim to *avoid* these problems is too strong, since it cannot be denied that some consciousness of latter-day authorities and theories informs all reading of the past. But this is a larger question which the approach taken by this book does not methodly invite, even though some readers might choose to ask it. Freud, to take an example, is indeed briefly discussed, but only in the specific context of Conrad's *Lord Jim*, with which his ideas might be thought to have some cultural and historical continuity. And this is the question that my account does raise as a function of its chosen method: how is it that modes of inquisition and even conclusions seem to be shared by different writers and genres when we cannot safely affirm that X borrowed directly from Y? In the search for an answer we commonly invoke the 'spirit of the age,' or make reference to some base phenomenon (for the Marxist it is economic, for the Hegelian a movement of universal mind) from which all priorities may be seen to be generated. I have tried to describe such a continuity rather than to account for it, tried to show the complexity and range of the ways in which the image or figure was seen as tending, materially and psychologically, to lapse into the fetish. The attribution of determination is deliberately not pursued in any way that limits speculation about exactly how history has worked, though I hope that there are plenty of hints for those who might wish to take them up.

I am grateful to Tony Tanner and to Penny Wilson for having read over most of the manuscript of this book; and to Edmund Leach, who provided me with a detailed bibliography of the history of fetishism as an anthropological concept, one that saved me, I suspect, many days of floundering and many oversights. Others among my friends and colleagues have provided continual stimulation and suggestions for further reading; among them, I would especially like to thank Penny Wilson, Colin MacCabe, John Barrell, Norman Bryson, and Michael Ignatieff. For valuable reactions at a time when this material was taking shape, I thank also Julia Tame, various friends and students at the Harvard Summer School, 1978, and for final suggestions, the reader for the Johns Hopkins University Press.

FETISHISM AND IMAGINATION

ABBREVIATIONS

BH: *Bleak House*
BR: *Barnaby Rudge*
DC: *David Copperfield*
DS: *Dombey and Son*
GE: *Great Expectations*
HT: *Hard Times*
LD: *Little Dorrit*
MC: *Martin Chuzzlewit*
NN: *Nicholas Nickleby*
OMF: *Our Mutual Friend*
OT: *Oliver Twist*

AF: *Almayer's Folly*
HD: *Heart of Darkness*
LJ: *Lord Jim*
N: *Nostromo*
OI: *An Outcast of the Islands*
TU: *Tales of Unrest*
V: *Victory*

CHAPTER 1

A WORLD OF IMAGES

Thou shalt not make thee any graven image, or any likeness of any thing that is in heaven above, or that is in the earth beneath, or that is in the waters beneath the earth.
Deuteronomy, 5:8

there are few of us, if any, who have not their own fetishes, or their own idols, whether in their churches, or in their hearts. . . .
F. Max Müller, *Lectures on the Origin and Growth of Religion*, 1878

CRUSOE BURNS AN IDOL

Towards the end of *The Farther Adventures of Robinson Crusoe* (1719) the hero is moving west across Asiatic Russia, finally intending to end his wanderings in the country of his birth. Entering the lands ruled by the Muscovites, he expresses relief at finding himself once again in a Christian country, and not one "where the People given up by Heaven to strong Delusions, worship the Devil, and prostrate themselves to Stocks and Stones, worship Monsters, Elements, horrible shaped Animals, and Statues, or Images of Monsters."[1] His belief is at odds with the facts, as so often before. He finds that there are another thousand miles of pagan territories, among which are interspersed "but an odd sort of Christians" (p. 177). These pagans prove to be the most barbarous in all his experience, except that they are not cannibals. He comes upon them worshipping an eight-foot-high "Block of shapeless Wood" decorated with devilish ornaments:

> I confess I was more mov'd at their Stupidity and brutish Worship of a Hobgoblin, than ever I was at any Thing in my Life; to see God's most glorious and best Creature, to whom he had granted so many Advantages, *even by Creation*, above the rest of the Works of his Hands, vested with a reasonable Soul, and that Soul adorn'd with Faculties and Capacities, adapted both to honour his Maker, and be honoured by him, sunk and degenerated to a Degree so more than stupid, as to prostrate it self to a frightful Nothing, a meer imaginary Object dress'd up by themselves, and made terrible to themselves by their own Contrivance; adorn'd only with Clouts and Rags; and that this should be the Effect of meer Ignorance, wrought up into hellish Devotion by the Devil himself; who envying (to his Maker) the Homage and Adoration of his Creatures, had deluded them into such gross, surfeiting, sordid and brutish things, as one would think should shock Nature it self.
>
> (Pp. 181–82)

The language may seem a little strong, even for a disappointed home-comer who had thought he was safely back to civilization. It emanates from a traditional Protestant polemic against the worship of graven im-

4

ages. For throughout all his exposure to alternative cultures Crusoe has kept his head and his faith, his views tainted by very little of that liberal open-mindedness to the relative truth-claims of strange anthropologies (and that corresponding scepticism about the authority of one's own) so commonly featured in eighteenth-century accounts of faraway places.

Crusoe's reference to the "gross, surfeiting, sordid and brutish" may be read as implicit evidence of his awareness of the idol as a phallic one. He has already told us that it has "no Feet or Legs, or any other Proportion of Parts" (p. 180). With missionary zeal, he tells us how he "rid up to the Image or Monster, call it what you will, and with my Sword cut the Bonnet that was on its Head in two in the middle, so that it hung down by one of the Horns" (p. 182). This causes considerable offense, and the Europeans are chased off. Not content, however, with this display of righteous indignation, Crusoe tries to persuade his companion to undertake a further punitive expedition: "I told him, I was resolv'd if I could but get four or five Men well arm'd to go with me, I was resolv'd to go and destroy that vile, abominable Idol, and let them see that it had no Power to help it self, and consequently could not be an Object of Worship, or be pray'd to, much less help them that offer'd Sacrifices to it" (pp. 182–83). The fellow traveler is more sceptical. He asks how the identity of the Christian God can possibly be communicated to people who already believe passionately in their own religion. Crusoe suggests destroying the idol at night and leaving a written message. But these people have no knowledge of writing, even in their own language. Further advised against the wider political expediency of such interference, Crusoe is yet undeterred. He persuades his companions to join him and, armed with gunpowder and good intentions, they steal into the village at night and burn the idol, having in good faith positioned some of its worshippers under duress nearby, that they may witness the inefficacy of their deity.

This almost starts a war. Hotfooting it for civilization, Crusoe and his party are caught by the pursuing Tartars. Instead of massacring the whole caravan without further ado, the 'barbarians' make an honest effort to discover the guilty persons: Crusoe himself, we may remember, has already shown his readiness to burn a whole village in revenge for the death of one man, in spite of his reservations about a similar incident in the past. But the Tartars are deceived by one of their own people in the pay of the Christians, and the party continues safely on its way.

Crusoe's behavior suggests that a lifetime of wandering among strange peoples has failed to convince him of the uselessness of such missionary ambitions, as it has also failed to introduce him to a sense of the relativity of all religions. It is also strangely at odds with the toleration he has formerly practiced in his own 'kingdom' towards his three subjects—one Protestant, one pagan, and one Papist (2.30–31). Further, at several points earlier in the narrative of his life and adventures (for example, 2.187f.)

Crusoe has gone to considerable lengths to record his high opinion of the character of the Spaniards, who as Papists might have been expected to come in for the same ferocious attacks on ornaments and idols as are directed at the Tartars. Protestant rhetoric against idolatry was frequently aimed directly or indirectly at Catholic rituals, but Crusoe seems anxious to point out the futility and wastefulness of disputes between the various forms of Christian faith.

I am not competent to decide, nor shall I take a guess, where Defoe himself stands on this question of idol burning. Perhaps Crusoe's function as the brainchild of a Dissenter is to try to heal the schisms within Christianity at the expense of all that is outside it, the true enemies of faith. Whatever the motive, Crusoe's behavior yet stands as a not unfamiliar form of crusading confidence. By way of a contrast, we may look at the conclusions of another fictionalizing traveler, Herman Melville. In *Typee* (1846) the narrator thus transcribes his first sight of the taboo-groves of the islanders:

> Beneath the dark shadows of the consecrated bread-fruit trees there reigned a solemn twilight—a cathedral-like gloom. The frightful genius of pagan worship seemed to brood in silence over the place, breathing its spell upon every object around. Here and there, in the depths of these awful shades, half screened from sight by masses of overhanging foliage, rose the idolatrous altars of the savages, built of enormous blocks of black and polished stone, placed one upon another, without cement, to the height of twelve or fifteen feet, and surmounted by a rustic open temple, enclosed with a low picket of canes, within which might be seen, in various stages of decay, offerings of bread-fruit and cocoa-nuts, and the putrefying relics of some recent sacrifice.[2]

The description is indeed invested with the standard contexts of paganism: gloom (moral as well as physical), silence, and foliage (dense forests and groves were traditionally identified with materialism—via the Greek pun on ὕλη—and hence with paganism). But as the narrator becomes more familiar with his new environment his estimation of the local religion changes. Though he finds the active meanings of the rituals "a complete mystery," he comes to be much less impressed by their seriousness:

> The festival had been nothing more than a jovial mingling of the tribe; the idols were quite as harmless as any other logs of wood; and the priests were the merriest dogs in the valley.
>
> In fact religious affairs in Typee were at a very low ebb: all such matters sat very lightly upon the thoughtless inhabitants; and, in the celebration of many of their strange rites, they appeared merely to seek a sort of childish amusement.
>
> (Ch. 24, p. 174)

He finds that, despite the "big and lusty images" of the taboo ground, the " 'crack' god of the island" is actually a small portable idol some ten inches high. The rites that go with the worship of this god, Moa Artua, are "like those of a parcel of children playing with dolls and baby houses" (pp. 174–77).

Two things in particular may be noted in Melville's treatment of pagan religion. First, he confesses anthropological ignorance about its exact function: "I saw everything, but could comprehend nothing" (p. 177). In this respect he identifies himself with a host of other bemused voyagers who had gone before him. Unlike Crusoe—and of course I am not suggesting a merely historical contrast here—he wants to find out; he is prepared to put aside his own predispositions to try to understand the workings of an alien theology. Second, and perhaps as a consequence of the above, he is able to see that, far from being mere passive worshippers of graven images, the islanders try to exercise an active control over their idols. If the desired effects do not seem to be following from their rites then the idols themselves are abused, receiving, in fact, according to the narrator's observations, "more knocks than supplications":

> I do not wonder that some of them looked so grim, and stood so bolt upright as if fearful of looking to the right or the left lest they should give any one offence. The fact is, they had to carry themselves *'pretty straight'*, or suffer the consequences. Their worshippers were such a precious set of fickle-minded and irreverent heathens, that there was no telling when they might topple one of them over, break it to pieces, and making a fire with it on the very altar itself, fall to roasting the offerings of bread-fruit, and eat them in spite of its teeth.
>
> (Ch. 24, pp. 177–78)

This second 'observation' (we should be uneasy with the word, since whatever Melville saw in the South Seas his book is much informed by accounts of other voyages) is particularly significant, for it inverts the representation of paganism put forward in *Robinson Crusoe*. Instead of mindlessly bowing down before their idol, as Crusoe reports the Tartars doing, the islanders see it as something over which they themselves exercise control. They seem not to have forgotten, as the Tartars had, that they have been the makers of the thing they worship. Further, there seem to be several idols open to various sorts of use and worship, not just one primary deity. To call these idols 'gods' in our sense of the word must then be something of a misnomer. They are far more open to persuasion and far more idiosyncratically personalized than one brought up in the Christian tradition might expect.[3]

Peculiarly enough, this seems to make the savages freer in their para-theological customs than are their more civilized observers. Earlier travelers had noted, for example, the apparent absence among South Sea islanders of any concept of an afterlife.[4] The effects of the supernatural are therefore strictly limited to life on earth. This freedom from the systematized impositions of a coherent theology affecting not only our behavior throughout this life, by a range of rewards and punishments, but also our

fate in the next, clearly appeals as an image of the innocence and sponta-
neity of primitivism. It accords with one of the obvious primary purposes
of *Typee,* the confusion of accepted standards of civilization and barba-
rism, along the lines anticipated by Rousseau and Diderot. It takes
nineteenth-century anthropology some time to recapture this image of the
paradisal alternative in paganism. It appears again in Frazer's *Totemism
and Exogamy* (1910), at a point where he corrects an opinion he had earlier
held. Totemism—which, as we shall see, is what replaces fetishism as a
more technical concept—is not a religion, and totems are not worshipped.
They are companionable objects, so that there is "an imaginary brother-
hood established on a footing of perfect equality between a group of people on the one side and a group of things . . . on the other side."[5] That is
a condition long since lost to European man.

As *Typee* offers a different version of the nature-culture antithesis, so its
narrator also condemns the Crusoe-like cast of mind:

> Let the savages be civilized, but civilize them with benefits, and not with evils;
> and let heathenism be destroyed, but not by destroying the heathen. The Anglo-
> Saxon hive have extirpated Paganism from the greater part of the North Ameri-
> can continent; but with it they have likewise extirpated the greater portion of the
> Red race. Civilization is gradually sweeping from the earth the lingering ves-
> tiges of Paganism, and at the same time the shrinking forms of its unhappy
> worshippers.
>
> (Ch. 26, p. 195)

Indeed, things are perceived as having gotten worse since Crusoe, whose
misguided act of faith does almost start a war, but who does not in fact
cause any of the Tartars to be killed. Melville, like other liberal consciences
in nineteenth-century America, has witnessed something approaching
genocide. The aggression that he identifies within the very aspiration to
"civilize" suggests that there is a less than wholly altruistic purpose to that
aspiration. A similarly complex idea of the colonial ambition, positioned
as it is along a spectrum of intentions ranging from mere greed to moral
idealism, is a leading subject in Conrad's novels.

There is a further version of the image of idolatry which is worth mentioning by way of introduction. At one point in *Mardi* (1849), that yet-
more-fictionalized travel story, the representation of the primitive seems to
have become largely a medium for commenting allegorically on the absurdities of the 'civilized' world as we know it. The Mardians are engaged
in ongoing and comprehensive despoiling of each other's idols: "While
one faction defaces the images of its adversaries, its own images are in like
manner assailed; whence it comes that no idol escapes" (ch. 111, p. 345). In
this world, the person who most profits from such a state of affairs is the
idol-maker:

> "When I cut down the trees for my idols," said he, "they are nothing but logs;
> when upon those logs, I chalk out the figures of my images, they yet remain logs;

when the chisel is applied, logs they are still; and when all complete, I at last stand them up in my studio, even then they are logs. Nevertheless, when I handle the pay, they are as prime gods as ever were turned out in Maramma."

(Ch. 114, p. 354)

With the insight that some people are making a healthy living out of fashioning images for others to worship, Melville touches on what I shall argue to be a dominant concern in nineteenth-century inquiries into the ethics of representation. In his conflation of the primitive with the civilized, and the implied ubiquity of the forgers of images, he seems to speak for a world in which there is no remaining recourse to a purer alternative. But for the most part, in the literature with which I shall be dealing, it is the white man's world that produces a far more energetic and comprehensive version of true paganism than anything to be found in the Pacific islands. Dickens, Melville, and Conrad are in various ways engaged in an analysis of this contemporary and intrinsic paganism.

FETISHISM AND IDOLATRY

Crusoe does not use the word *fetish* in any of his tirades against the worship of graven images. The word was certainly available to him (*OED* records it from 1613 onwards), but it had a rather technical sense until the nineteenth century, often relating specifically to religious practices in West Africa.[6] In the nineteenth century, however, it frequently seems synonymous with *idolatry* in the polemical 'protestant' vocabulary directed against the endowing of inanimate objects with values and powers which properly belong to human states of mind and feelings. As such, it takes on a much wider range of references outside the anthropological, and comes in fact to suggest itself as the word or concept most suited to describe the operations of a misguided and miscreating society.

Both the word itself, and the syndrome it describes, become important in Romantic models of perception as ways of specifying what must be avoided in individual acts of representation and in the social interactions based upon them. I have elsewhere described the historical situation whereby, in Wordsworth's poetry and in the context of moral and theoretical speculation to which it relates, *all* perception had come to be regarded as fundamentally figurative.[7] The mind operates not by registering a mirror image of a world of substances outside it, which can then be equated with a shared world of realities and objects, and relations between objects, but by a selective process whereby certain images, which are the products of sense data recomposed by the mind within such limits as are established both by its mechanical structure and by its individual and social predispositions, are assembled into wholes. These wholes are, by the useful activities of language and/or conceptual intelligence, both put about for social consumption and exchange, and redetermined by them.

These are not philosophical novelties original to Romanticism, of course. Similar ways of explaining the mind's processes of perception had in fact dominated the models of English philosophers throughout the seventeenth and eighteenth centuries. Nor was it the Romantics who for the first time put forward the idea that the mechanics of perception allow for crucial deviations into misrepresentation. Similar issues are, for example, raised in the famous aphorisms from the first book of Bacon's *Novum Organum*. Discussing the four kinds of *idola* (a translation of the Greek εἴδωλα, meaning "images" or "representations," passing conveniently via the Latin into the English word *idol*, with all its implications of falsity and deceit), Bacon enumerates four modes of misunderstanding occasioned by the operations of the senses in the visible world. Roughly speaking, these pertain (1) to the species as a whole (the limitations of our means of perceiving), (2) to the individual (whether physiological idiosyncrasy or learned behavior), (3) to the interaction of men in society (for example by language), and (4) to the false methods and philosophies hitherto passed off as true.[8] These types of *idola* seem not to be logically distinct—types 2, 3, and 4 might collectively redetermine each other and presumably type 1—but to serve rather as differently emphasized inhibitions on the achievement of truth.

What does, however, seem to be unusually critical in Romanticism is the scope admitted for misrepresentation and disagreement in the mind's *habitual* operations. (Though we may take Hobbes's *Leviathan* to respond to a similar urgency about consensus, occasioned by the Civil War.) If all perception is figurative and selective, then universality can only be maintained as long as it is assured or assumed that all people share the same modes of selection. Romantic discourse is conversely emphatic about the constitutive importance of what is *not* shared, or at least cannot be assumed to be. The natural and the normal are destabilized, seen as the products of particular figurations, whether of individuals or of limited social groups. When society is seen to be composed of different interests, and when interest helps determine perception, then it cannot be taken for granted that what is 'seen' by one person will be the same as what is 'seen' by another. This is a theory of disagreement, an articulation (whether a priori or a posteriori, determining or derived) of the clashing of mutually ignorant armies in the dark.

Romanticism presents many versions of this situation and many suggestions for its solution. If the construction of reality is selective and influenced by interest, then a radical democracy obtaining among seers would be one way of preventing the encoding of any particular configuration as the privileged one. There must then be no assumption of the 'natural.' This is indeed what we find in the aesthetics of Blake, Wordsworth, and

Shelley. Coleridge, perhaps more prophetic of things to come, tries to incorporate an egalitarian spirit into a reconstituted and reenergized hierarchy wherein an authentically learned class passes on to others the results of the processes of its own education into self-consciousness. Offered in this way, the products may again become processes for those who are able to take the hint and to provide the necessary cocreative energy.

Such hopeful solutions are, I think, less evident in the reflections of later writers on the balance of freedom and inhibition in the individual and social imagination. Such writers often suggest, I shall argue, a series of *impasses* developing from the modes of representation characterizing the social groups they observe. These are at times described, and almost always conceivable within, the vocabularies of idolatry and fetishism.

The dominant feature of an idol or a fetish—and I shall discriminate between the two in due course—is that, by being a material embodiment of a human aspiration or motive, it tends by the very fact of its objective form to cause its creator or employer to forget that he is himself responsible for its creation or continued existence. This operates both for the individual consciousness in isolation, and of course for any other minds on whom an already created idol or fetish is imposed. In the first case it results in self-suppression and the abdication of basic responsibilities; in the second it becomes a potential tool working for the hegemony of one individual or faction. These two modes of alienation are not exclusive, of course; quite the opposite. Dickens presents those who (like Mr. Dombey) profit from fetishizing others as themselves fetishized. They are themselves excluded from the authentic and creative human satisfactions of which they deprive others.

Fetishism is a dangerous potentiality in all perception and representation precisely because reality itself is open to construction. Thus do metaphors pass into realities. Coleridge, quoting Bacon, begs and demands that man should be purified of the "arrogance" which leads him "to take the forms and mechanism of his own mere reflective faculty, as the measure of nature and of Deity. In this indeed we find the great object both of Plato's and of Lord Bacon's labors. They both saw that there could be no hope of any fruitful and secure method, while forms, merely *subjective*, were presumed as the true and proper moulds of objective truth."[9] In a passage describing the dangers attendant upon causal thinking, itself necessary as "the condition under which alone experience and intellectual growth are possible," he further points out the social consequences of such individual misapprehensions:

> By the same law, he [mankind] is inevitably tempted to misinterpret a constant precedence into positive causation, and thus to break and scatter the one divine and invisible life of nature into countless idols of the sense; and falling prostrate before lifeless images, the creatures of his own abstraction, is himself sensual-

ized, and becomes a slave to the things of which he was formed to be the con-
queror and sovereign. From the fetisch of the imbruted African to the soul-
debasing errors of the proud fact-hunting materialist we may trace the various
ceremonials of the same idolatry, and shall find selfishness, hate and servitude as
the results.

(The Friend 1.518)

The connection between the anthropological paradigm and the immediate situation is forcefully made. It is close to the process that Kant had
called "subreption," or the "substitution of a respect for the Object in
place of one for the idea of humanity in our own self—the Subject."[10] And
in *The Prelude* Wordsworth adverts to the same syndrome in distinguish-
ing Coleridge himself from those who remain the slaves

> Of that false secondary power, by which,
> In weakness, we create distinctions, then
> Deem that our puny boundaries are things
> Which we perceive, and not which we have made

and in marking out his poem as not for those of us

>   who are fed
> By the dead letter, not the spirit of things,
> Whose truth is not a motion or a shape
> Instinct with vital functions, but a Block
> Or waxen Image which yourselves have made,
> And ye adore.[11]

Here again is the concern expressed so frequently in Romantic thought;
that the reciprocal interchange of inner and outer developing through
time, and made necessary by recognizing the mind as fundamentally figurative in its operations, has been arrested, and fixated at the outward pole.
The world 'lives' only as the mind itself remains lively and creative of
changing forms, shapes, and motions.

This confusion of product with process, or matter with spirit, was invoked by Dulaure as the misunderstanding central to the ancient religions,
their error consisting in the idea that "the sign, the figure, or the symbol
had the same force, the same supernatural power, and the same benevolent
or protecting faculties as those which were attributed to the sacred object
thus figured or symbolized; that the sign was worth as much as the thing
signified."[12] In this context he accepts an extended definition of fetishism
which includes not just things but also words: "Thus all things, and even
all words, spoken or written, to which one attributes a miraculous force
foreign to their essence and contrary to the laws of nature, must belong to
fetishism" (1.33–34). There was some argument about whether this use of
the term was too extensive, and some writers of (what we now call) anthropology were anxious to limit its reference in order to make clear distinctions between fetishism and other pagan forms of worship such as sabe-

ism, heroism, and idolatry. Arguments about vocabulary, and about which particular variant was the origin of the others, can be found all over the literature on the subject.[13] De Brosses had also advocated an extended use covering all cult objects endowed with divine power, be they animal, vegetable, mineral, or sidereal (pp. 10–11, 18–19). Meiners, too, for whom fetishism is the oldest and most universal form of worship (1.143), also takes over an extensive usage of the term. De Brosses does, however, preserve a distinction between fetishism and idolatry. Idolatry preserves a residual consciousness that what is worshipped is only represented by, and not embodied in, the idol; fetishism is a step further down the ladder in that it worships things as and for themselves (p. 64). This is why Dulaure regards fetishism as historically prior to idolatry, the latter developing out of the former when conscious attention moves from things in themselves to things as representations of the human form (1.454 f.); he entertains, it seems, the idea that the mind has made progress through historical time. But the distinction, at least, became familiar, and was thus taken over, by F. Max Müller: "A fetish, properly so called, is itself regarded as something supernatural; the idol, on the contrary, was originally meant as an image only, a similitude or a symbol of something else."[14]

The idea of a historical development out of fetishism, whereby the mind has gradually educated itself out of the lower forms of materialism toward a greater degree of spiritual insight, is one that appealed to the more optimistic apologists of culture, and indeed to many anthropologists. But for many users of the vocabulary, idolatry and fetishism were identified as equally deadening in their hold on contemporary life, and consequently as good as synonymous (see, for example, Coleridge, *The Friend* 1.106). They are the more threatening for being merely the most reductive and inert extremes of a habit of mind which in its higher manifestations was held to be absolutely essential. Coleridge had declared that poetic images are characteristic of genius "when a human and intellectual life is transferred to them from the poet's own spirit,"[15] thus commending a process already derided by Hume:

> There is an universal tendency among mankind to conceive all beings like themselves, and to transfer to every object, those qualities, with which they are familiarly acquainted, and of which they are intimately conscious. We find human faces in the moon, armies in the clouds; and by a natural propensity, if not corrected by experience and reflection, ascribe malice or good-will to every thing, that hurts or pleases us.[16]

This habit is particularly common among poets, Hume says, and even philosophers are sometimes guilty of similar lapses, as when they ascribe "to inanimate matter the horror of a *vacuum*, sympathies, antipathies, and other affections of human nature." De Brosses says much the same thing in his account of fetishism:

> We know that man has a natural tendency to imagine beings similar to himself, and to suppose in external things the qualities which he experiences in himself. . . . The practice of personifying such things, whether into physical or moral beings, is a metaphor natural to man, whether in his civilized or primitive condition.
>
> (Pp. 215–16)

In the same sense, man,

> forced by fear to suppose the presence of invisible powers, and led by the senses to fix his attention on visible objects, has synthesized two opposed and simultaneous operations, in attaching the invisible power to the visible object, without distinguishing, in the crude state of his reasoning, between that material object and the intelligent power that he supposes there.
>
> (P. 217)

These are the habits of mind that lie behind fetishism, some degree or ramification of which, for de Brosses as for Hume, is common to all ages and cultures. We can see the coincidence between the above detailed habits of mind and Romantic epistemology and aesthetics, which maintain that insofar as the mind is making meaning then it is employing phenomenal figures, shared or otherwise, to do so. Fetishism thus becomes a particular condition of a process that typifies and constitutes all efficiently meaningful thought. Self knows itself only by reflection upon what is other, and that 'other' is a result of a perceptive mechanism in which the self has already played a creative part. Thus it is that healthful figurative activity had to be carefully distinguished from fetishism within the same model of the mind's operations. Here is Wordsworth on the human imagination:

> These processes of imagination are carried on either by conferring additional properties upon an object, or by abstracting from it some of those it actually possesses, and thus enabling it to re-act upon the mind which hath performed the process, like a new existence.[17]

Seeking echoes or mirrors of itself, perhaps; and even if more generous than this, it is only *continual* creation and reaction which save such gestures from inertia, and hence from fetishism. That "new existence" must be consciously held as a figure by the mind which made it, and never worshipped in itself.

In a passage from *Home at Grasmere* Wordsworth describes the refining effects of anthropomorphism under ideal limiting conditions in small communities. Feelings are first ascribed to objects from motives of individual selfishness or self-regard, but accruing collectively through time these humanized objects come to generate feelings of love,

> And giving to the moments as they pass
> Their little boons of animating thought,
> That sweeten labour, make it seem and feel
> To be no arbitrary weight imposed,
> But a glad function natural to Man.[18]

What maintains the line between healthy imagination and fetishism is the insistence on the *changeful* nature of familiar experience, and on the oscillation between activity and passivity in the mind, which is thus never enduringly either master or slave. In the observation that such imaginative attributions serve to "sweeten labour" we may note a threatening prospect for the fate of labor within a fetishized society; more of this later. For the moment, the emphasis is on the "animating thought" that ensures the primacy of the activity of mind over the claims of the thing to 'reality' status. By contrast, among the various ways of reading "A slumber did my spirit seal," we can infer a fetishistic ingredient in the speaker's past behavior:

> She seemed a thing that could not feel
> The touch of earthly years.
>
> No motion has she now, no force;
> She neither hears nor sees;
> Rolled round in earth's diurnal course,
> With rocks, and stones, and trees.[19]

The reproof by the alerted consciousness may have come too late to make amends. The subject may indeed now be dead, as she had before been imaged out of her lively complexity of joy and pain into a fixed form beyond the reach of time and change. Whether the motive was one of adulation (for example of a lover or a child), or merely a laziness of mind designed to preempt the need for attentiveness, the gesture seems to be related to fetish worship. As such, its true tendency is indeed toward death, which is the only ultimate fixity able to be posited from within the experience of life, and which seems to be intimated in the second stanza of the poem.

Similar moments of correction are to be found in others among Wordsworth's poems, often explicitly invoking the images of idols and fetishes. The rape of nature chronicled retrospectively in "Nutting" (*Poetical Works* 2.211–12) took place when the youth had made himself into

> a Figure quaint
> Tricked out in proud disguise of cast-off weeds
>
> (Ll. 8–9)

and was in a mood when

> of its joy secure,
> The heart luxuriates with indifferent things,
> Wasting its kindliness on stocks and stones,
> And on the vacant air.
>
> (Ll. 40–43)

The erring youth is here partaking of the same vices as Crusoe's Tartars who had worshipped the same "stocks and stones." He is not authentic; he has borrowed his clothes, for decoration rather than need, much as bad poets have borrowed their diction. He is in a state of luxury rather than essential subsistence. These details are presented as contributing to the misdeeds and misconceptions which follow vis à vis the world of natural things.

If this were to be another book about Wordsworth or Romanticism, which it is not, then much more would have to be said about the usefulness of the vocabulary of fetishism and idolatry as a way of making clear the concerns implicit in the poetry of Wordsworth and his earlier contemporaries. Geoffrey Hartman, in his analysis of "The White Doe of Rylstone" and the conclusion to his *Wordsworth's Poetry, 1787–1814* (New Haven: Yale University Press, 1964, pp. 324–38), has much to say about the complexity of Wordsworth's attitude to personification and imaging, reciprocally processes in the human mind and objects standing before it. For Hartman, "The White Doe" "attempts to distinguish between a basically superstitious and a more humane attitude toward the symbols or second natures which we 'participate' " (p. 327); between, in other words, a form of fetishism on the one hand and a revivifying imaginative engagement on the other. The same discrimination might also inform a reading of "The Thorn," or help to articulate some of the problems readers often experience with "The Old Cumberland Beggar" and its confrontation with the way in which charity, like pity, may divide the soul. Coleridge's ancient mariner might also be described as gradually freeing himself from a fetishistic cycle of adoration and destruction, replacing it by a more generous and properly subjective identification through love; or, so he tells us. But, as I say, this is not to be a book about Romantic poetry, though it does mean to show the way in which the Romantic aesthetic is adapted into the consciousness of the following generations.

The fear of idolatry and fetishism as elements existing potentially in all perception may be explained from another angle, that of Protestant theology. De Brosses observed that personification had not come to an end with the age of reason (p. 7), and he noticed the particular tendency of fetishism to become incorporated into contemporary forms of behavior: "These irrational practices do not disappear in a country in proportion as reason gains sway there: above all when they are sanctified by inveterate custom and by pious credulity . . . they even mix themselves with other dominant cults, and more recently established dogmas" (p. 186). He is in fact talking about ancient Egypt, but it is hard not to sense a reference beyond. Comparisons of the ancients and the moderns, or of savages and civilized peoples, in terms of the relative degrees of idolatry in their various customs were not uncommon.[20] Voltaire, for example, in the article on "Idolatry" in the *Philosophical Dictionary*, had argued strongly against the smugness that dismisses ancient religions as idolatrous; he thereby at once preserves the integrity of the ancients and refuses any easy contrast between paganism and Christianity. Idolatry always exists in the eye of the beholder as a term of abuse: "The Moslems who filled Greece, Asia Minor, Syria, Persia, India and Africa, called the Christians idolators, *giaours*, because they believed that the Christians worshipped images. They smashed several statues they found in Constantinople in Santa Sophia, in the church of the holy apostles, and in others which they converted into mosques."[21] Idolatry is everywhere and nowhere. Each faction or faith sees it in its rivals and uses it as an excuse to persecute or destroy them. In this light Crusoe's idol burning seems a little unjustified. The ancients were no more idolatrous than are the moderns:

> It is evident that the priests attached as much divinity as they could to their statues in order to attract more offerings to themselves. We know that the philosophers condemned these superstitions, that the warriors made fun of them, that the magistrates tolerated them, and the people, always absurd, did not know what it was doing. This, in a few words, is the history of all the nations to whom god has not made himself known.
>
> (P. 247)

In other words, the history of us all. But Voltaire's cultivated and tolerant scepticism was not as widespread as enlightened reason might seem to demand. Crusoe's behavior did emanate from a firmly held conviction in the 'Puritan' mind about the worship of outward forms. Though Crusoe himself does not voice any animus against Catholicism, the availability of the vocabulary of fetishism for a convincing critique of Popery was too tempting to be missed for many writers in the Protestant tradition. Carlyle wrote of the Puritans as "men intent on the real essence of things" engaged in a struggle against "men intent on the semblances and forms of things."[22] Coleridge accused Catholicism of encouraging attention to "refracted and distorted truths, profound ideas sensualized into idols, or at the lowest rate lofty and affecting imaginations, safe while they remained general and indefinite, but debased and rendered noxious by their application in detail."[23] In response to an earlier debate, Locke also had decided that Catholics were idolaters, idolatry being defined as "performing outward worship . . . before an image, where either the place, time, or other circumstances give the spectator reason to presume that one is employed in some act of religious or divine worship."[24] And, in a sonnet on the revival of Popery composed as part of a sequence retelling centuries of English history, Wordsworth speaks of the people again embracing their "Gods of wood and stone" (*Poetical Works* 3.377).[25]

We may turn to Kant for an extended statement of this polemic, and for a very precise use of the vocabulary of fetishism to convey it. "Fetishism" in religion occurs when a worshipper "labors under the illusion that he possesses an art of bringing about a supernatural effect through wholly natural means."[26] Kant perfectly captures here that element of coercion which the sharper-eyed travelers had noticed in the Pacific islanders' behavior toward their deities. Such desires are totally outward oriented; the fetishist believes he can work *upon* God to accomplish that which is beyond his own powers (pp. 165–66). There is no reference to inward morality, which is for Kant the core of authentic religious experience. He goes on to argue that all obedience to "statutory laws" or institutions as things in themselves rather than simply as *means* to a "moral disposition" amounts to *"fetishism"* (pp. 166–67). All forms of "clericalism" are open to such an accusation, and "however few the imposed observances, so long as these are laid down as unconditionally necessary the faith remains a fetish-faith through which the masses are ruled and robbed of their moral freedom by subservience to a church (not to religion)" (p. 168). Correspondingly, religion becomes "idolatry" when a worshipper substitutes reverence for God as an external being for self-conscious attention to "morally upright conduct on earth" (p. 173). Even silent prayer partakes of these corruptions when it consists merely in a petition for something to be done without one's own exertions (p. 183).

This is an extreme application of the polemic against the worship of graven images and the unreasoned respect for inherited forms. The location in the Protestant consciousness of this suspicion of outward, materialized representations is not irrelevant, for it identifies this strong current in nineteenth-century thought as having implicitly religious sources and analogues. Wordsworth, for example, stands within a theological tradition when he voices a moral outrage against "the bondage of definite form; from which the Hebrews were preserved by their abhorrence of idolatry" (*Prose Works* 3.34). He refers here to the Hebrew conviction that earthly things should never be used to represent divinity, lest the material vehicle come to supplant the spiritual reality in the minds of its users. Hume had made the same reference in mentioning the universality of the propensity towards idolatry:

> And of this, some theists, particularly the JEWS and MAHOMETANS, have been sensible; as appears by their banishing all the arts of statuary and painting, and not allowing the representations, even of human figures, to be taken by marble or colours; lest the common infirmity of mankind should thence produce idolatry.
>
> (*Essays* 2.335)

Coleridge also often cites the Hebrews in exactly this context,[27] but if we turn to Hegel's comments on the subject we can see that there is a problem in the Hebrew mode as a paradigm for imitation:

> The *negative* relation, on the other hand, of sublimity strictly so called, we must seek in Hebrew poetry: this poetry of sublimity can celebrate and exalt the imageless Lord of heaven and earth only by using his whole creation as merely an accident of his power, as the messenger of his sovereignty, as the praise and ornament of his greatness, and in this service by positing even the greatest [earthly] splendour as negative.[28]

This obviously poses a problem for those who would communicate the identity of the divine principle. The poet (in this case) must use partial, limiting forms to excite the mind of his hearer, but in such a way as to demand reference back to the wholeness in which the parts have their life and purpose. The question is, how can this be done without incurring the risk of fixation upon the part, which would then become a species of idolatry or fetishism? This task informs Romantic theory in a thorough and widespread way. The whole cannot be represented except by parts, as the appeal of known forms is a necessary means of stimulating the mind. Coleridge tries to come to terms with a similar problem in his theory of the "symbol," wherein each item invoked for the purposes of representation must be seen to stand for and within the whole from which it comes. In the case of the Hebrew paradigm, however, that whole would have to be the entire creation, and the reiterated invocation of this entireness would leave no room for the exercise of those other faculties with which Coleridge was constantly preoccupied: the conscience and the will. This has much to do, I think, with his reaction to Pantheism, and with the maturing recognition that Protestant man must never forget that he lives with the consequences of the Fall. Any recourse to wholeness must therefore be provided only through the realities of work and effort.

The theological context as here adduced thus provides a model for explaining (as it may also indeed have in some sense caused) the middle ground that Romantic theory always tries to maintain between the terror of absolute formlessness and the obverse prospect of fetishism. Both extremes threaten to remove the play of change and balance, which is the natural occupation of the fallen mind as it explores the possibilities for choice and reconciliation, thereby discovering its own conscience. The Fall in this way becomes inextricably fortunate, not the least of its consequences being the pleasures (and difficulties) of poetry. Wordsworth makes the point in his analogy between poetry and religion:

> The concerns of religion refer to indefinite objects, and are too weighty for the mind to support them without relieving itself by resting a great part of the burthen upon words and symbols. The commerce between Man and his Maker cannot be carried on but by a process where much is represented in little, and the Infinite Being accommodates himself to a finite capacity. In all this may be perceived the affinity between religion and poetry; between religion—making up the deficiencies of reason by faith; and poetry—passionate for the instruction of reason; between religion—whose element is infinitude, and whose ultimate trust is the supreme of things, submitting herself to circumscription, and reconciled to substitutions; and poetry—ethereal and transcendent, yet incapable to sustain her existence without sensuous incarnation.
>
> (*Prose Works* 3.65)[29]

Pure, imageless contemplation of the deeper truths is impossible for our ailing senses. Because of this, we occupants of the middle ground are committed to a state of perpetual watchfulness. Effort and labor are everywhere called for; in the poet, as he tries to confirm the integrity of his own relation to form and image, and in the reader, who must be prepared to accept the task of cocreation in the production of pleasure and enlightenment. Without such efforts, the poet becomes a narcissistic figure of power, and the reader is condemned to a state of mind in which his aesthetic dormancy, his theological impropriety, and his political passivity are all reciprocally assured.[30] Coming home to the Lakes from Cambridge, a world that shows "The Idol weak as the Idolater" (*The Prelude* 3.638), Wordsworth finds his own attitude to nature threatened by contagion: the "great frame of breathing elements" has become a "senseless Idol" (4.303–4). *Fetish* is a common term of moral disapprobation in Carlyle, and an even commoner one in Arnold's *Culture and Anarchy*, where it is reiterated time and time again as the image of a fixed and mechanical respect for the outside of things, of dead ideas that are passionately held to, of the "stock notion" or "mechanical maxim," and of all things that inhibit the "free and fresh stream of thought."[31] Coleridge remarked, "Could we emancipate ourselves from the bedimming influences of custom, and the transforming witchcraft of early associations, we should see as numerous tribes of *Fetish-Worshippers* in the streets of London and Paris, as we hear of on the coasts of Africa" (*The Friend* 1.106). Dickens, I shall be contending, transcribes the doings of those fetishists.

TRINKETS AND BAUBLES

One frequently noticed version of what I have been calling 'fetishism' is the worship of ornament. It attracted particular censure from the critics of fetishization, and was related to dangerous trends in both imaginative and economic life. Ornament is related metonymically to that which it decorates or adorns. It does not belong to its object except by coincidence or contiguity, as the scepter to the king or the ring to the finger. Thus, insofar as the ornament comes to function as a sign representing the thing to which it is habitually connected, any attention to that sign as a thing in itself partakes of fetishism. There is of course another factor explaining the particular urgency of the polemic against ornament. Being decorative, it appeals to its beholders and possessors on imaginative and aesthetic grounds as well as on those of representative convenience. It is seen as pleasing, and people are naturally inclined to attend to images that give pleasure. Robes and furred gowns do indeed hide all, but so does sackcloth. Utility alone does not explain the choice between them.

In an important letter to Wilberforce, apparently written early in 1801,

Wordsworth delivers a synoptic statement about the negative effects of the worship of outward forms:

> When the material forms or intellectual ideas which should be employed to [rep]resent the internal state of feeling, are made to claim attention for their own sake, then commences Lip-worship, or superstition, or disputatiousness, in religion; a passion for gaudy ornament and violant stimulants in morals; and in our literature bombast and vicious refinements, an aversion to the common conversational language of our Countrymen, with an extravagant preference given to *Wit* by some, and to outrageous *incident* by others; while the most sacred affections of the human race seem to lay no hold on our sympathies unless we can contemplate them in the train of some circumstances that excite *curiosity*, or unriddle them from some gaudy phrases that are to attract our wonder for themselves.[32]

Religion, morality, literature, and language are here related in a demand that such attention to external signs or vehicles should never be sustained without continuing reference to the inner creative powers that should have constructed them in the first place. The sight of an image must always call up the *act* of representation, without which all processes of social and personal regeneration must cease. The famous argument against "poetic diction" belongs in the context of this case against ornament. As Wordsworth describes it, it is poetic diction that (like the London theaters) offers an image divorced from a reality, tempting us by its surface coruscations to exercise on language alone the powers that properly belong to the feelings and passions. Like the fetish, such improper language seeks to inhibit the reference back from sign to signifying act; and, like the fetish, the more ornamental and decorative it is (the more tricks, enigmas, and hieroglyphs it employs), the less we suspect any authentic origin in the powers within.[33]

Plainness, conversely, is the required feature of a language designed to offer itself only as a pointer to its own processes of coming into being, which is what Wordsworth always seeks to point his reader toward. In this sense his argument is firmly within an ongoing tradition of moral debate in the eighteenth century. John Gordon, for example, writing anonymously in 1762, had maintained that, "In an age of ornament, the aim of every one will be, rather to exhibit the little he knows with shew and ostentation, than to examine into the principles, on which it is founded. For this purpose the grand object of his attention will be language."[34] In such a "refined" language,

> words cease to be regarded as the representatives of things; and are so far from carrying the mind on to any farther contemplation, that they rather invite it to stop at them alone; forming, as it were, a specious kind of skreen between us and nature; which we must either throw down, or turn our eyes some other way, if we would obtain a true view of things. And the more exquisite the painting on

> this skreen appears, the more it will attract our regard, and the less likely shall
> we be to divorce ourselves from it to look on the rougher and less polish'd face of
> nature.
>
> (Pp. 39–40)

The Puritan vocabulary rings through once again. All things painted, graven, or fabricated are to be placed in doubt. By them we are persuaded to fix on "the shell instead of the substance" (p. 56), that is to become fetishists or worshippers of externals. Against a conventional tradition representing the classical authors as exempla of robust simplicity of manners (if not always of expression), Gordon argues that they were in fact more prone to such "false painting" (p. 77) than the moderns. Poetic language aside, however, he is quite emphatic about the disastrous propensity of his contemporaries toward ornament and away from "natural simplicity" (p. 43).

Probably more familiar to Wordsworth was the case against ornament made by Godwin:

> Garlands and coronets may be bestowed on the unworthy, and prostituted to the intriguing. Till mankind be satisfied with the naked statement of what they really perceive, till they confess virtue to be then most illustrious, when she most disdains the aid of ornament, they will never arrive at that manly justice of sentiment, at which they seem destined one day to arrive. By this scheme of naked truth, virtue will be every day a gainer; every succeeding observer will more fully do her justice, while vice, deprived of that varnish with which she delighted to gloss her actions, of that gaudy exhibition which may be made alike by every pretender, will speedily sink into unheeded contempt.[35]

Godwin too wishes to subsist as "a man speaking to a man" (2.55), and in his terminology here we can see all the images of theatricality which Wordsworth also employs to invoke deceitful representation: varnishing, gaudiness, gloss, and so forth. Disavowing ornament and insignia, Godwin is also discrediting metonymy, which even when authentic is implicitly reductive of what it represents. The king, for example, if he be a worthwhile king, is hardly summed up by the throne or scepter. At the same time, such images are very obviously open to misuse; anyone can sit on the throne, grasp the scepter, and call himself a king.

It is not simply the case that these sign systems are more open to misuse than others; insofar as they are inessential, they also commit their users to a condition of self-alienation. In opting for the metonym or ornament, the wearer or bearer has been fixed at the 'outward' pole of the axis of representation. He no longer exercises control, in other words, over how he represents himself; the signs have become part of a public discourse (by which he is known), and can be then reciprocally reimposed back upon him by an achieved consensus in which he, as an individual, may no longer wish to take part. This situation to a degree affects all signs when they become part of a language or communication system, but it is particularly important to the metonym because its relation to the human subject is inessential, and therefore most unfitted for enduring attachment or respect. Ought we not to give up our badge of office more readily than our right arm, by all standards of good sense?

At the same time, like so many of the more threatening aspects of experience, the function of ornament and attribute is located firmly within the middle ground of universal human behavior, so that it must always be negotiated by the strenuous conscience. Kant specified such images as fundamental to human nature, both for their communicative efficiency and their aesthetic appeal:

> A regard to universal communicability is a thing which every one expects and requires from every one else, just as if it were part of an original compact dictated by humanity itself. And thus, no doubt, at first only charms, e.g. colours for painting oneself (roucou among the Caribs and cinnabar among the Iroquois), or flowers, sea-shells, beautifully coloured feathers, then, in the course of time, also beautiful forms (as in canoes, wearing-apparel, etc.) which convey no gratification, i.e. delight or enjoyment, become of moment in society and attract a considerable interest.
>
> (*Critique of Judgement* 1.155–56)

However, if the ornamentation is introduced contingently, "introduced like a gold frame merely to win approval for the picture by means of its charm," then it is mere *"finery"* and detracts from "genuine beauty" (1.68).

One tenant of the middle ground was, once again, Wordsworth, and there is an interesting account of one of his 'lapses' in the recollection of his journey to chapel in the Cambridge book of *The Prelude*.[36] I shall not go into great detail here, but it is worth mentioning as a precise instance of the ambivalent reaction to ornament I have specified as typical of life between two extremes, fetishism and formlessness. The ornament in question is the surplice, the badge of distinction and the sign of permission which the young Wordsworth has to wear as a member of his college. This surplice is a "dislocated lump" (l. 316) over his shoulder, a disjoined and disjoining sign of which he is half proud and half ashamed, "gloried in, and yet despised" (l. 318). It is imaginatively and perhaps aesthetically appealing, but also morally disapproved of, as an image setting the wearer apart both from the "plain Burghers" looking on and from his own essential self. Ornament and plainness are here the features of a division within society, and the bearer of the ornament is defined by it before he has had a chance to exercise his own powers of figuring and imaging. His rôle preempts the development of his individuality.

Perhaps significantly, this articulate confusion of reactions and convictions is experienced immediately after the young Wordsworth has been drinking excessive toasts to Milton in Milton's old college rooms. Inebriation has made him lose track of time, hence his hurry back to chapel. Warmed by an imagined contact with that stern presence, it is perhaps not to be wondered at that "the rites" (l. 315) which at once reclaim him should seem "unworthy vanities" (l. 328) divisive of man from man.

The most pervasive examples of metonymic representation tended (then as now) to be drawn from the trappings of state, and in particular of monarchy. For some radical writers, like Godwin, monarchy was the frailest and most deceitful of all figurings taken as reality, and the most disastrous reduction of the many to the one. By drawing all power "to a single centre" (*Enquiry* 2.33), monarchy is potentially the most fetishistic form of government. (Although Godwin does not use the word *fetish*, he is analyzing the obsessive concentration on a single person or image, before which all self-dependent power is abdicated.) That monarchy is also untruthful is indicated for Godwin in its use of the lowest form of figuring, the metonymic:

> To conduct this imposture with success, it is necessary to bring over to its party our eyes and our ears. Accordingly kings are always exhibited, with all the splendour of ornament, attendance and equipage. They live amidst a sumptuousness of expence; and this, not merely to gratify their appetites but as a necessary instrument of policy. The most fatal opinion that could lay hold upon the minds of their subjects, is that kings are but men. Accordingly, they are carefully withdrawn from the profaneness of vulgar inspection; and, when they are shown to the public, it is with every artifice that may dazzle our sense, and mislead our judgment.
>
> (2.49–50)

The point had been made at even greater length and with even more direct philosophical insight by Ferguson:

> When, amidst circumstances that make no trial of the virtues or talents of men, we have been accustomed to the air of superiority, which people of fortune derive from their retinue, we are apt to lose every sense of distinction arising from merit, or even from abilities. We rate our fellow-citizens by the *figure* they are able to make; by their buildings, their dress, their equipage, and the train of their followers. All these circumstances make a part in our estimate of what is excellent; and if the master himself is known to be a pageant in the midst of his fortune, we nevertheless pay our court to his station, and look up with an envious, servile, or dejected mind, to what is, in itself, scarcely fit to amuse children; though, when it is worn as a badge of distinction, it inflames the ambition of those we call the great, and strikes the multitude with awe and respect.[37]

The insight here is precise; if we are brought up in a world where the figure counts for the real, we tend to be unable to tell the difference. Thus we "think we are talking of men, while we are boasting of their estates, their dress and their palaces" (p. 252); we have "transferred the idea of perfection from the character to the equipage," and this fiction is, with a bitter irony, itself reciprocally directed back at the 'real' to redefine it in terms of its own needs. The whole structure of labor and effort is now focused on the maintenance of something imaginary, as the "pageant" of public position is "adorned at a great expence, by the labours of many workmen" (p. 253).

This is, clearly enough, a form of fetishism, in the broader sense of the word. The thing endowed with value and inviting envy is in itself "scarcely fit to amuse children," but it becomes the focus of immediate attention and also of subsequently active and energetic meditation. There is a passage in Wordsworth's *A Guide Through the District of the Lakes* which may be read in the light of this concern about man-made things usurping the attentions that might properly be directed at more essential or 'natural' objects. Wordsworth starts out by excusing the building of gentlemen's mansions, a permission which does not at first sight accord with the polemic against artificiality so important in his writings generally. And in fact, the limiting conditions that he imposes serve to emphasize that polemic once again. Such mansions should be built only in locations where there are *no* dominant natural forms (such as mountains) which they might rival or replace in the attentions of the eye in the landscape. In the absence of alternatives, the mansion might then stand as a kind of substitute for the absent natural form, "and, itself being a work of art, works and traces of artificial ornament may, without censure, be extended around it, as they will be referred to a common centre, the house" (*Prose Works* 2.214). Artifice is allowed where it grows out of an a priori artificiality. But these houses must never be built among mountains proper, where they might be "obtruded in rivalship with the sublimities of Nature." Lack of observance of this caveat has resulted in the "disfigurement which the Country of the Lakes has undergone." The tendency for culture to absorb and refigure nature after its own image must be checked, as here, by a conscious refusal of planning permission.[38]

The owner of the kind of mansion described above would exercise an influence on his society not unlike that of the monarch within the commonwealth as a whole. He, signified by his house, is the center to which all eyes and minds subtend, the "common centre" of his world. He is the possessor of power and influence, and the figure he puts forth is an expression of that power, an invitation to others to look upon it, perhaps to worship it. Dupuis, another analyst of fetishism in the literal sense, makes exactly this point about the priesthood: "It is above all by means of statues and images that priestly imposture exercises its power over credulous mortals, and develops all the resources of the art of influence."[39] The operations in large, homogeneous, and 'civilized' societies of processes analogous to fetishism and idolatry are therefore much more dangerous than they might be in, say, the villages of West Africa, where plurality tended to be recognized as of the very essence of fetishism, and where each person might have his private object of worship, with the many not being reduced to the one.

By contrast, Godwin describes countries such as Britain, where

> every thing is uniform: the ceremony is all, and the substance nothing. In the riots in the year 1780, the mace of the house of lords was proposed to be sent into the passages, by the terror of its appearance to quiet the confusion; but it was observed that, if the mace should be rudely detained by the rioters, the whole would be thrown into anarchy. Business would be at a stand; their insignia, and, with their insignia, their legislative and deliberative functions, would be gone. Who can expect firmness and energy in a country, where every thing is made to depend, not upon justice, public interest and reason, but upon a piece of gilded wood?
>
> (*Enquiry* 2.54–5)

There are two absurdities to be grasped here, that the mace might indeed have quelled the riot and that, had it not done so, its loss would have disjoined power from its habitual possessors. Godwin means us to infer that such power has no proper basis, and the passage quoted here in fact describes a situation where neither those who are subject to authority nor those who apparently possess it are in control of the language of social exchange. The 'thing' has taken over as beyond them both. Ferguson saw this to be the fundamental paradox of privilege, whereby the aristocrats are "at once the servants and the masters of the state" (*Essay*, p. 68). The sovereign too, as he inspires fear in others, "has abundant reason to give this passion a principal place with himself . . . from his eager desire to secure, or to extend, his power, he finds it become, like the fortunes of his people, a creature of mere imagination and unsettled caprice" (p. 71). That is to say, by the extension of what is already insubstantial to ever-greater claims, a realization of the frailty of the figure ensues. What has been naturalized can always be questioned and reduced to its original imaginary status, and the person wielding the scepter must tend to recognize that the metonyms are more important than the man that holds them. He himself, that is to say, becomes a signifier for the content of the *rôle* which he occupies; he is himself a figure, and he has only figures to sustain him.

Marx puts this very clearly: "Determinations of reflexion [Reflexionsbestimmungen] of this kind are altogether very curious. For instance, one man is king only because other men stand in the relation of subjects to him. They, on the other hand, imagine that they are subjects because he is king."[40] The situation is thus one of pure differences, whose insubstantiality the course of direct experience must always threaten to reveal. Hegel had made much the same comment in the context of the analysis of the name:

> Through the name the power is the monarch. Conversely, he, this particular individual, thereby knows himself, *this* individual, to be the universal power,

knows that the nobles not only are ready and prepared for the service of the state power, but that they group themselves round the throne as an *ornamental setting*, and that they are continually *telling* him who sits on it what he *is*.[41]

Each reciprocally posits the objectivity of the other by identifying it (or him or them) with some reified intermediary signifier; name, throne, or scepter. It is the 'ornament' or insubstantial sign (the name) which holds people apart from reprocessing their relations in renovating ways. We cannot 'speak' to a 'king.'

We shall see in Dickens's novels that the alienating function of the name may operate in the service either of self-protection or of conscious or unconscious deceit. Some characters cannot afford to announce who they are and, like Captain Nemo in *Bleak House*, adopt pseudonyms. Others disguise themselves (whether by taking false names, like John Harmon in *Our Mutual Friend*, or by cultivating tics and obsessive traits, like Newman Noggs in *Nicholas Nickleby*) because they cannot bear to or afford to confront the world with their true natures; for reasons that may be privately or socially enforced, they experience a fear of any direct discourse. Finally, some characters reveal a positive ambition to identify themselves with outward attributes, as a way of getting on in the world and being noticed by it. Mr. Turveydrop (*Bleak House*) comes to mind here, as he names his son "Prince" in wishful connection with the Prince Regent, thus imposing on him an alienated identity from the start.

What the name does in these specific contexts is to disjoin image from identity, always with the threat that image will subsume identity through the very power of its social significations. This is exactly what 'ornaments' in general were thought to do. Godwin regarded the manufacture of "trinkets and luxuries" as the least essential use of human labor. This industry would be the first to disappear if the national economy could ever be directed away from surplus and back to subsistence production (*Enquiry* 2.482). At the same time, he saw in the imperfect society around him an obsessive preoccupation with the emblems of difference and distinction:

> If we survey the appendages of our persons, there is scarcely an article that is not in some respect an appeal to the good will of our neighbours, or a refuge against their contempt. It is for this that the merchant braves the perils of the ocean, and the mechanical inventor brings forth the treasures of his meditation. The soldier advances even to the cannon's mouth, and the statesman exposes himself to the rage of an indignant people, because he cannot bear to pass through life without distinction and esteem.
>
> (2.426–27)

In his own generation, he goes on, the most popular means of pursuing such esteem is the "exhibition of wealth" (p. 427). This results in the creation of a false system of values, one typified by the usurpation of the inner by the outer qualities, which is exactly what Smith had complained of in

The Theory of Moral Sentiments; "wealth and greatness" are accorded the attention properly belonging to "wisdom and virtue," one of the results of which is that "the external graces, the frivolous accomplishments of that impertinent and foolish thing called a man of fashion, are commonly more admired than the solid and masculine virtues of a warrior, a statesman, a philosopher, or a legislator."[42] Smith mounts an argument in which the need for approbation is the motive that makes man pursue wealth and power, signs of identity. This is paralleled by his insight into the inessential nature of the *things* that exhibit them to others. Such objects are ultimately unsatisfying for the person deploying them; they do however encourage the recirculation of wealth, which is the ideal prospectus held out by the argument of *The Wealth of Nations*. Smith tries to show that wealth expended on "durable commodities," even when they are "frivolous objects, the little ornaments of dress and furniture, jewels, trinkets, gewgaws" and the requirements of a "base and selfish disposition,"[43] is inevitably going to circulate to some degree because it involves paying a manufacturer to produce them. The same argument is used to describe the passage from a feudal to a commercial society (pp. 417ff.). But the individual thus spending his wealth is giving way to "the most childish vanity" (p. 422) in this pursuit of "trinkets and baubles" (p. 421), and is ultimately committing himself to the experiences of infinitely deferred gratification and frustration.

The importance of ornament in these formulations of Godwin and Smith clearly has an economic function. It is desire for ornaments and inessentials which (following one explanation among others) creates the imperative to move from subsistence to surplus economies. If you have more than enough to eat, you can exchange some of the surplus for what you 'want.' This issue belongs in the context of an absolutely central eighteenth-century debate, reflected all through its literature, about the origins and effects of luxury. I shall not try to develop the case here.[44] Suffice it to say that there was a strong tradition identifying luxury as dangerous to social organization and civic virtue. In Rousseau's words, luxury is "like those scorching winds, which, covering the trees and plants with devouring insects, deprive useful animals of their subsistence and spread famine and death wherever they blow."[45] Once again, the argument against luxury draws upon the Puritan vocabulary of plainness and simplicity. Gordon makes this clear in a passage equating luxury with ornament in language, inessential commodities with superfluous rhetoric, both generative of a habit of fashionable craving and desire:

> The introduction of ornament into the world of letters, is just like the introduction of Tea, Coffee, Sugar and Spicery, into the world at large: it will run from the sailor's wife up to my Lady Duchess; and from thence down again to the dirtiest dish-washer in her Grace's back kitchen: every body will be fond of it;

and every body, except those who think, will sacrifice every thing that is useful for the sake of it.

(Occasional Thoughts, p. 51)

That elements of surplus are criticized both in language and in the national economy suggests a common identity for the moral priorities that thus criticize. It can be found in what I have described as the 'Protestant' suspicion of the dangerous effects of the hegemony of outward forms, tending as they do toward fetishes.

The disposal of a surplus, of course, creates not just a movement of wealth within the state (wherein it is seen to break down the divisions of rank and class within that state, as in the Gordon passage cited above), but also a pattern of foreign trade. Looking at the narratives of eighteenth-century voyagers, one notices that ships tended to carry for exchange, not utilities or necessities, but the trinkets and baubles that they imagined would appeal to the 'primitive' mentalities of their hosts. I have come across no account of the reasons for this, though I would be surprised if there were not a comment on it somewhere. Maybe such trinkets were easier to carry. Or perhaps there was an assumption that ornaments would prove a more successfully universal standard of exchange than the specific utilities required by the different societies to be visited. Given that the obsession with ornaments was also being theorized as a contemporary European disease, and moreover theorized in the vocabulary of paganism and primitivism, perhaps the reexportation of useless objects to the parts of the world wherein they were thought to be original is not to be wondered at. Whatever the reasons, the narratives do report some interesting cases of cultural conflict arising out of this European preoccupation. Cook, for example, finds that instead of *creating* a market for trinkets and frivolities, as he seems to have assumed he would (according to some universal theory of specious appetite?), he has already almost exhausted it: "Some of the natives would not part with a hog, unless they received an axe in exchange; but nails, and beads, and other trinkets, which, during our former voyages, had so great a run at this island, were now so much despised, that few would deign so much as to look at them" (*Voyage* 2.10). Even more tellingly, de Bougainville relates the events of a meeting with a native of the Moluccas: "He came up to our boat without shewing any marks of fear or surprize. Our people asked him for something to eat and to drink, and he offered them water, and a small quantity of a sort of flour, which seemed to be his ordinary food. Our men gave him a handkerchief, a looking-glass, and some other trifles of that sort. He laughed when he received these presents, and did not admire them. He seemed to know the Europeans. . . . "[46] The European races have built their empires on such transactions, and it is a melancholy episode that thus shows their habits and assumptions demystified. The handkerchief is an attribute of 'civilization,' the tool for making away with the unseemly sweat of the brow, the nasal discharges of cold climates, and perhaps the tears of excessive emotion. In the looking glass, European man superimposes the image of the self on that of the other. Rousseau was theorizing the difference between the likes of this native of the Moluccas and the vagrant Europeans in a way that helps to explain the misunderstanding (itself, of course, a part of discourse as much as it is a factual observation): "The savage lives within himself, while social man lives constantly outside himself, and only knows how to live in the opinion of others, so that he seems to receive the consciousness of his own existence merely from the judgment of others concerning him. . . . We have nothing to show for ourselves but a frivolous and deceitful appearance. . . . " (pp. 220–21). Imaged, perhaps, in handkerchiefs and looking glasses. "He seemed to know the Europeans." That chorus will resound, albeit hopelessly, in Conrad's novels of the colonial experience. Conrad is even more interested in analyzing the fetishism within the European imagination. Consequently, such moments of potential correction as those described here become even rarer and even more ineffective.

COMMODITIES AND MONEY

Still by way of introduction, there is another element in nineteenth-century discourse which needs to be seen within the context of the fetishized imagination: the commodity, and its chosen universal form, money. By putting it this way I do not mean that the commodity must be understood in this way as a universal, ahistorical fact. The point is that the *theory* of the commodity was situated within the spectrum of concern over the hegemony of outward images commonly known as "fetishism." The explicit connection that Marx (famously) makes between the commodity and the fetish therefore emerges coherently and intelligibly out of a historical predicament and preoccupation.

The commodity is a form of fixing and representing, for the purposes of storage and exchange, processes of human labor which in themselves are evanescent and not open to representation except by something they have made. Smith makes this clear in his distinction between manufacturing and other forms of labor:

> The labour of the manufacturer fixes and realizes itself in some particular subject or vendible commodity, which lasts for some time at least after that labour is past. It is, as it were, a certain quantity of labour stocked and stored up to be employed, if necessary, upon some other occasion. That subject, or what is the same thing, the price of that subject, can afterwards, if necessary, put into motion a quantity of labour equal to that which had originally produced it. The

labour of the menial servant, on the contrary, does not fix or realize itself in any particular subject or vendible commodity. His services generally perish in the very instant of their performance, and seldom leave any trace or value behind them, for which an equal quantity of service could afterwards be procured.

(Wealth of Nations, p. 330)

Fixity and realization are here envisaged as means of storing labor, representing in stable forms or images something that, properly speaking, cannot be fixed or arrested, and must therefore be imaged into some more pliable form. The contrast is between the requirements of developing capital and the situation whereby the contract between worker and employer has to be perpetually reestablished, because the labor involved creates products that "perish in the very instance of their performance."

The idea of continual dissolution and creation was, as we know, a principle of great importance to the theories of the imagination as they are found in the writings of Shelley, Blake, and Wordsworth, and its aesthetic vehicle was the unstable interaction of mind and world. The idea of metaphor in *A Defence of Poetry*, for example, depends upon no single relation between differences ever being able to encode itself as the 'real.' By analogy with what Smith has to say about the commodity, it might be said that Shelley's idea of the poetic element of language falls somewhere between the two extremes typified by menial and manufacturing labor; it rebels against being fixed in the way that the commodity is fixed, but yet it does not entirely disappear as a repository (in writing) of the relations that it came into being to express. The written word remains as potentially creative of future relations, as well as expressive of old ones; the old are continually slipping away as the new arise. In Shelley's formulation, language occupies the 'middle ground' in a way that is not open to the forms representing human labor. Every item within it can be living image or dead metaphor, according to the states of mind and imagination of its users and receivers. What happens with the commodity, however, is that its makers cease to be important as soon as the making is finished. For 'meaning' to be conveyed no reference need ever be required back to the process through which the commodity came into being, whereas it is in the nature of language and of the faculties of mind through which it functions that such reactivation should, at least occasionally and with the appropriate stimulus, occur.

As the commodity is a means of fixing and storing labor in order to produce something that is available for exchange, so wealth is the product of the control of commodities. This ties up with what I have already said about the imaginary investment in display, in a way that is here perceived by Ferguson. As man is "the great storemaster among animals," so

He finds in a provision of wealth, which he is probably never to employ, an object of his greatest solicitude, and the principal idol of his mind. He appre-

hends a relation between his person and his property, which renders what he
calls his own in a manner a part of himself, a constituent of his rank, his condition, and his character, in which, independent of any real enjoyment, he may be
fortunate or unhappy; and, independent of any personal merit, he may be an
object of consideration or neglect; and in which he may be wounded and in-
jured, while his person is safe, and every want of his nature completely supplied.

(*Essay*, p. 12)

In doing so, he suggests both the nature of the investment and the possible
reasons for it. The accumulation of wealth goes far beyond the requirements of need, partly as a means of achieving status in a world where
figures count for everything, and also partly because such figures function
as a protection from the discomforts of new, unfixed experiences. It is the
body, or the person, which hides behind the figure, which then bears the
brunt of the negative aspects of the social relation as well as bringing about
the desired ones. But there is a price to pay for this abdication from risk and
personal responsibility: loss of the real, of "real enjoyment" as well as real
pain. Mr. Dombey will discover this loss only after his son has died and can
no longer be enjoyed.

Ferguson here touches on the double motivation behind what we are
calling 'fetishism,' that it is inspired by an aspiration toward control
which is based on fear: fear of the unpredictability of experience. This
unpredictability and its capacity to dislocate habit had been a positive
thing for Wordsworth, for whom a degree of instability was the vehicle of a
moral education. He had sought to disturb the figurative faculty at exactly
the moments when it was threatening to establish a closed relation of static
correspondence between mind and world, eye and object. Always of course
intimidated by the full sublimity of absolute dissonance, he nevertheless
tried to publicize an appreciation of the positive effects of an instability
experienced in the middle range of a spectrum completed by fetishism at
one end and total formlessness at the other. This is the area in which the
poet's imagination is least destructive of the self and prospectively most
available as a paradigm for other imaginers, and in which it can function
as a barometer of social and individual well-being in relation to a ferment-
ing nature.

Ferguson's "great storemaster," conversely, is inhibited from experiencing any disturbance of his habits, hiding as he is behind the disguise that
he has chosen (or has been obliged to choose) as constitutive of his very
identity. Ferguson's analysis suggests the essentially social genesis of the
apparently private compulsion toward the accumulation of wealth and
property. The urges for supremacy and protection are both a consequence
of an individuality that recognizes itself in being recognized by others. It is
Marx, of course, who most fully and famously carries through the analysis
of this, and relates it explicitly to the vocabulary of fetishism. Commodities are "sensuous things which are at the same time suprasensible or
social":

The commodity-form, and the value-relation of the products of labour within which it appears, have absolutely no connection with the physical nature of the commodity and the material [dinglich] relations arising out of this. It is nothing but the definite social relation between men themselves which assumes here, for them, the fantastic form of a relation between things.

(*Capital*, p. 165)

The analogy is with religion, where "the products of the human brain appear as autonomous figures endowed with a life of their own"; and this legitimizes his invocation of the term *fetishism*. Its incidence is inseparable from the appearance of the commodity itself.

A similar abdication of the ongoing responsibility for the figurative takes place in the specific case of money, which begins as a "mediating activity," but then comes to be seen as the real power over what it thus mediates. Once again man loses control and worships his own invention:

Its cult becomes an end in itself. Objects separated from this mediator have lost their value. Hence the objects only have value insofar as they *represent* the mediator, whereas originally it seemed that the mediator had value only insofar as it represented them.[47]

This is a motivated misattribution, of course, for money is an extension of the commodity in its capacity for, apparently, 'storing' labor. As such it is the mechanism of social division, and Marx makes this clear in another analogy with religion, one that appears very like a socialized version of the mind-world relation basic to Romantic epistemology:

The more man puts into God, the less he retains in himself. The worker puts his life into the object; but now his life no longer belongs to him but to the object. Hence, the greater this activity, the more the worker lacks objects. Whatever the product of his labour is, he is not.

(3.272)

In a wage economy, needless to say, the worker does not have much choice about subscribing to his own supersession. Money becomes not only a way of replacing the instability of the labor process, always potentially uncontrollable in being alive, but also a way of committing the worker to a smaller scale version of the same compulsion. In *Past and Present* Carlyle describes how money can thus contribute to the "extinction of the moral sense in large masses of mankind":

The symbol shall be held sacred, defended everywhere with tipstaves, ropes and gibbets; the thing signified shall be composedly cast to the dogs. A human being who has worked with human beings clears all scores with them, cuts himself with triumphant completeness forever loose from them, by paying down certain shillings and pounds. Was it not the wages I promised you?

(*Works* 10.194)

Money, like metaphor, affects both terms of the relation, both sides of the exchange. It gives common focus to the relation of employer and worker.

It alters the quality of both the independent people who use it. As such, it may be seen in terms of the Romantic concern for authentic exchange, which it denies.

But money is much more subversive than metaphor, which is at best creative. The Coleridgean imagination "dissolves, diffuses, dissipates, in order to recreate" (*Biographia* 1.202), operating upon what is given in order to bring its *own nature* forward for self-consciousness. And in so doing, it remains a faculty of the *mind*, being "essentially *vital*, even as all objects (*as* objects) are essentially fixed and dead." Money, for Marx, also effects relations between disparate things, but in such a way as to create material forms for fetish worship, turning the figured into the real, the metaphoric into the literal, and taking away the chance for its employer to recognize the exclusively *human* responsibility for the functioning of terms of exchange:

> It converts my wishes from something in the realm of imagination, translates them from their mediated, imagined or desired existence into their *sensuous, actual* existence—from imagination to life, from imagined being into real being. In effecting this mediation, [money] is the *truly creative* power.
>
> (*Works* 3.325)

This kind of creation, of course, is miscreative. We are no longer talking in abstractly ethical terms of a tyrant eye whose subversiveness consists in its separation of man from man at a spiritual level, but of a figured form that has the terrifying power to construct the real in crudely material ways, and ways that must seem to others objective and unarguable. From its beginnings in a kind of impotence on the subject's part, money becomes a tool for building up the world of one's wishes, or at least the semblance of it. So solid are the forms in which it deals that there is nothing to remind its possessor of the essential lack of control on which its very existence is based. It turns *"reality into a mere image"* (p. 325), and produces "the world upside-down—the confounding and confusing of all natural and human qualities . . . it is the fraternisation of impossibilities. It makes contradictions embrace" (p. 326). Like excessive wit and metaphor for an earlier generation, it yokes "heterogeneous" things "by violence together";[48] it turns all things to their opposites, accomplishing the "universal confounding and distorting of things: impossibilities are soldered together by it" (p. 324). And, like metaphorical expressions, the embodying of process as product, labor as commodity, demands in those who experience it an analysis of the figure or image which reads back to its original genesis. As Wordsworth demands reference back from words to the passions and feelings which created them as vehicles for exchange, so commodities appear as naturalized objects requiring a similar activity of deciphering. Here is Marx on the capital relations devolving from the labor process:

Reflection on the forms of human life, hence also scientific analysis of those forms, takes a course directly opposite to their real development. Reflection begins *post festum*, and therefore with the results of the process of development ready to hand. The forms which stamp products as commodities and which are therefore the preliminary requirements for the circulation of commodities, already possess the fixed quality of natural forms of social life before man seeks to give an account, not of their historical character, for in his eyes they are immutable, but of their content and meaning.

(Capital, p. 168)

Wordsworth, it will be remembered, had stressed the need that poetry shares with religion for a "sensuous incarnation" (*Prose Works* 3.65) making it available to a community. But the commodity comes into existence in a much more thoroughly reified situation. In the eyes of those who employ it and are employed by it, it is "immutable," a "natural form" whose analysis must precede any new access of political and spiritual creativity. In this context, Wordsworth's analogy is beset not only by the possibility that the relation between spirit and incarnation might not be perceived in similar or controllably connected ways by different people, but also by the even more fundamental problem that the *need* for such a relation might not be seen at all. This is what is threatened by the accession of the figure to the status of a "natural form." Marx, of course, would insist that there are those who have a vested interest in not encouraging the activation of such a relation.

In the case of money, this vested interest applies to us all, since it cannot be desirable or convenient to reconvert money back into the plurality of commodities whose mutual incompatibilities it has come into being to resolve. As money is yet further removed from the labor process (or from any other authentic values with which it might be conflated) than the commodity, being in fact the commodity form *of* commodities, so its hold over the mind is potentially even stronger.

Smith's comments on money in *The Wealth of Nations* are interesting in this context, for they focus exactly on the way in which the money form subverts the distinction between the organic and the mechanical. The advantage of money as a commodity is that it is "less perishable" than most, and can "be divided into any number of parts, as by fusion those parts can be easily re-united again." Thus the person who wants to buy a small amount of salt, but has only an ox to offer in exchange, is obliged either to buy more than he wants or to dismember his ox (p. 39). In the money economy, this inconvenience is avoided by making the easily divisible pieces of metal stand for the parts or part of the animal, as of whatever else its owner possesses. The piece of money as metonym represents the part of the animal, which is inseparable from the whole to which it belongs. Another (useful, of course) confusion of kinds takes place as the money form separates out use value from exchange value; water is highly useful, but has little or no exchange value, whereas in the case of diamonds the exact opposite is true (pp. 44–45). Money may make us forget that the one should ultimately lead us back to the other, as indeed it does when exchange becomes compulsive for its own sake, with no reference to necessities. Commodities, of which money is one, began as modes of storing labor, but "though labour be the real measure of the exchangeable value of all commodities, it is not that by which their value is commonly estimated" (p. 48). We forget that commodities are the products of signifying activities as much as they are things in themselves: "The one is a plain palpable object; the other an abstract notion, which, though it can be made sufficiently intelligible, is not altogether so natural and obvious" (p. 49). And even money, which expresses the relative exchange value of commodities, does so exactly "at the same time and place only" (p. 55).

Smith is therefore anxious, in his ideal economy, to insist on the reference back from the figure of money to the reality of labor and production:

> The gold and silver money which circulates in any country may very properly be compared to a highway, which, while it circulates and carries to market all the grass and corn of the country, produces itself not a single pile of either. The judicious operations of banking, by providing, if I may be allowed so violent a metaphor, a sort of waggon-way through the air; enable the country to convert, as it were, a great part of its highways into good pastures and corn fields, and thereby to increase very considerably the annual produce of its land and labour. (P. 321)

Smith's own theories detailing the need for approbation provide evidence for the use of wealth for quite other purposes. To invoke the same violent metaphor, there are those who spend their money on appearing to good effect on the highway, that they may be seen approaching from afar. They do not leave the road to attend to their fellows in the fields, even if part of their wealth does find its way back by indirect means.

In itself nothing, the identity of money should consist in its use as a means of exchange and distribution. Allied with the power of fantasy and future-oriented speculation, however, its possessor is tempted to begin a cycle of 'saving for the big one' which is never-ending. John Brown expresses this problem in a way which anticipates the whole gallery of misers peopling nineteenth-century fiction:

> The Passion for Money, being founded, not in Sense, but Imagination, admits of no Satiety, like those which are called the natural Passions. Thus the Habit of saving Money, beyond every other Habit, gathers Strength by continued Gratification. The Attention of the whole Man is immediately turned upon it; and every other Pursuit held light when compared with the Increase of Wealth.[49]

The more insubstantial the real, the more space there is for the imaginary. Even that luxurious spending on trinkets and baubles which Smith saw as (ideally) stimulating some level of recirculation is here inhibited.

Conversely, when money does circulate, the apparent universality of its influence and efficiency leads its users into another temptation. As the form of exchange in which all other forms and qualities may be expressed or imagined, it becomes subversive of remaining spheres of authentic human reciprocity. As Marx put it, "Assume *man* to be *man* and his relationship to the world to be a human one: then you can exchange love only for love, trust for trust etc." (*Works* 3.326). When you can pretend to "buy" love or trust, then things are badly awry, as they seem to be in the following equation, by Bentham, of capital with the essential passions of pleasure and pain. Money is "the most accurate measure of the quantity of pain or pleasure a man can be made to receive":

> The pleasures which two men will be deprived of, by being made to lose each a given part (suppose a tenth) of their respective fortunes, will in *specie* perhaps be very different; but this does not hinder but that, on taking into the account quantity on the one hand, and actual expectations and probable burthens on the other, they may be the same; they will be the same as nearly as any two quantities can be made to be so by any rule of measuring. It is from his money that a man derives the main part of his pleasures; the only part that lies open to estimation.[50]

There is an argument here which should not be slighted: Bentham is saying that money is the only way in which *comparative* pleasure may be reasonably estimated on a social basis. There may be other pleasures, but they cannot be measured one against another. But we can still see the dangers of this way of arguing as it misses out the full statement of the processes whereby such discordant things come to be seen in the same light. The hints or assumptions that all men would regard money in the same way, and that the most important forms of pleasure may be gained through money, would have horrified Wordsworth as they were to horrify Dickens.

It should not be forgotten that, if money indeed partakes of the qualities of the fetish, then it is a highly efficient way of organizing the exchange processes in a diversified and populous society. If we have enough of it, then there is open to us a high correlation of what we *want* with what we can have. But it can also be argued that money does not provide—that in fact it destroys—what we most *need*. In a sense it both attracts and distributes fetishistic energies; it is a thing that promises the acquisition of other things, things that can be bought. Something of the innocence of original fetish worship has here been lost. De Brosses (pp. 52–53) tells the story of a Cuban tribe that came to regard gold as the "fetish" of the invading Spaniards. Thus, when they heard of the approach of the fleet, they gathered together all their gold into a basket in order to celebrate the fetish, to obtain its protection, and to make it go away from their island: "They danced and sang around the basket, according to their religious conventions, then they threw it into the sea" (p. 53). This innocence obviously takes the writer's eye. It was probably lost on the Spaniards. Gold to them was not a simple fetish, with whom a continuing metaphysical interaction had to be maintained in order that it *might* impart protection and good fortune. It was not open to dismissal when its powers failed, for there was little evidence of its ever *having* failed. It was the basis of a money system, and as such it was efficiently convertible into an intended reality with the minimum of trouble. The tyrant eye has in money a very efficient tool in its task of making the world after a desired image. Money is the perfect image of desire, 'being' nothing, and promising everything, forever. It is a fetish that it is therefore all the more difficult to disassemble.

CHAPTER 2

CHARLES DICKENS: "NOTHING BUT FIGURE"

*It were, in our opinion, an offence against humanity to place Mr.
Dickens among the greatest novelists. For, to repeat what we have
already intimated, he has created nothing but figure. He has added
nothing to our understanding of human character.*
Henry James, review of *Our Mutual
Friend*, in *The Nation* 1, 21 November 1865

QUESTIONS OF COAT AND WAISTCOAT

Henry James, like many of the great critics, allows the motivations behind his objections to appear. "Nothing but figure" is indeed an apt description of the world that Dickens creates, and it is true that the dominance of the figured precludes the portrayal of what James means by "human character." But we should not follow James in ascribing this fact to a failure of observation on Dickens's part. In saying this, James seems to assume that all people will see the same world if they only open their eyes, and that what he himself sees before him is the true world, which Dickens could have seen if he had only paid attention. This assumption bypasses a whole emphasis in the Romantic and post-Romantic tradition which makes 'reality' itself a construct, a function of habit and disposition in conjunction with the basically selective mechanisms of perception in the human brain. It bypasses the notion that 'seeing' is not the transcription of a stable, unchanging world but the result of a predisposed configuration, whether elected or imposed. It ignores an important debate about the analysis of the 'natural.' James does not convey a view of perception and communication as functions critically implicated in audiences and motivations, and in the specific moments of history, both discursive and material.

It is true that Dickens is not for the most part writing the kind of novel in which the complex analysis of what James calls "character" plays a large part. As such his novels are indeed a refusal of the kind of universality intimated in James's comments. Character for him has *become* "figure." The recitation (always itself a kind of construct) of the operations of intimately described and deployed mental states, which is what many readers think of as "character," is not an option that Dickens's writing seems to mean to permit us. Instances occur, of course, and there are certainly protagonists who have what we might think of as an inner life, but the general direction and emphasis is away from the implications of subjective flexibility and free will which tend by the very energy of complexity to accompany the transcribed modulations of a sophisticated consciousness. Central observers who are in control of the narrative, like Pip and David Copperfield, do of course demonstrate an inner life, but it is ironized, often being presented very much in terms of the depths that are *not* there, even though it would be better if they were. In general, Dickens's writing functions through a comparative elision of the reader's opportunities for speculating on the workings of a 'rounded' consciousness. Individuality is very much a social construct, and the construction of society is heavily dominated by negative modes of seeing and imaging.

The novels can be read as investigations of the subsumption of the *possibility* for "character" (as James defines it) by already created images and figures. Once in place, these attract and deaden the energies of whatever creative aspirations are born into their world. Dickens thus chronicles the *energetic* creation of deadness and fixity, the passionate reduplication of fetishized representations. It can be the need for self-protection which creates people who have become mere figures, compelling them into obsessive concentration on one personality trait or attribute; but the way this pressure operates is through the human imagination itself, as if it were a 'willed' reduction of variety to singleness. Thus we find protagonists who seem to be frightened of the kind of unmediated, undeflected language of human exchange which Marx calls for, "trust for trust" (*Works* 3. 326), for reasons which might seem entirely personal—shyness in love, or fear of controversion, for example. At the same time, these personal decisions exist in a context where indirection is the norm, and where open self-expression can even be dangerous. At this point the whole possibility of separating individual and social determination becomes questionable; each is the other. The subject is objectively determined, and reciprocally determines the objective.

It would not be overstating the case to say, I think, that in this respect Dickens presents consciousness itself as historical. This represents a more restricted world than that of the earlier Romantics. Even though we can see in Wordsworth the intuition of a sociohistorical theory of mind, or at least of perception and of the ethical faculties that relate to it, there remains always a sense that the imagination can at best break through the constraints (this ability itself of course is a consequence of a certain way of life) to create radically unpredictable orderings and new directions, new figures. It must be said that these new makings are largely private, or able to be shared only with the smallest societies; but with Dickens the reliance upon the human heart is commonly effected only by the most extravagant flouting of the privileges of fiction. It is this extravagance that has led to Dickens being judged a sentimental or an improbable writer. To answer this, we need only remember that he is responsible for the tangled plots that *make* the improbable resolutions necessary. The manipulation of providence becomes itself a signal of the chaotic disjunctions of a world without it; the fiction encourages a negative inference about what is really the case, even as it provides the gratification of an alternative.

Dickens perhaps for the first time writes the world that Schiller's pessimistic vision had forecast, one wherein we see "whole classes of men, developing but one part of their potentialities," and individuals as "fragments . . . with the result that one has to go the rounds from one individual to another in order to be able to piece together a complete image of the species."[1] Perhaps the Dickens world is even gloomier for, by and large, the assembly of fragments produces no such thing as a complete image. People are not simply divorced *from* society; there is no such organic body for them to belong to. There is no "symbolic" representation, in the Coleridgean sense, because there is nothing there to be represented symbolically.

Coleridge died in 1834. The year before, a book had been published which can be seen as one of the most brilliant and penetrating anticipations of Dickens's concern with the disjunctive aspects of figurative representations and images, and the consequent incidence of fetishism. Carlyle's *Sartor Resartus* is a prolonged and rather serious jeu d'esprit on the subject of clothes. "Nothing but clothes," James might have said. Carlyle investigates the "vestural Tissue. . . . which Man's Soul wears as its outmost wrappage and overall; wherein his whole other Tissues are included and screened, his whole Faculties work, his whole Self lives, moves, and has its being" (*Works* 1. 2). As all barbarous men desire clothing, so it seems that all men are in this respect barbarous: "The first spiritual want of a barbarous man is Decoration, as indeed we still see among the barbarous classes in civilised countries" (p. 30). Note that Carlyle says that the want (which is both lack and desire) is "spiritual"; it has little to do with need of the most basic kind, but embodies a certain inward aspiration and provides a mode of social exchange which is nothing less than a "language": "Clothes gave us individuality, distinctions, social polity; Clothes have made Men of us; they are threatening to make Clothes-screens of us" (p. 31). The outward sign, itself only in an imaginary relation to what it represents, subverts and reconstructs (or dissolves) the inner identity: "reaching inwards even to our heart of hearts, it tailorises and demoralises us" (p. 45). Like Godwin and Ferguson, and Wordsworth in his analysis of the signifying effects of the upshouldered surplice, Carlyle sees the function of the attribute as constituting the mystification of identity into difference.

Teufelsdröckh's "manuscript" is a wide-ranging assessment of a contemporary preoccupation with the outward, which is seen to relate directly to the Kantian philosophy and its distinction between phenomena and noumena, or things as they appear and as they are thought to be in themselves. As this theory intimates that what is seen is all merely surface, so are all earthly codes and institutions open to analysis in the light of the "Science of Clothes," which must then take, must it not, scientific rank beside Codification, and Political Economy, and the Theory of the British Constitution; nay rather, from its prophetic height looks down on all these, as on so many weaving-shops and spinning-mills, where the Vestures which *it* has to fashion, and consecrate and distribute, are, too often by haggard hungry operatives who see no farther than their nose, mechanically woven and spun?

(Pp. 215–16)

We are to note, with some cynicism, the presence of a class excluded from the enjoyment of these vestural systems, whilst being essential to their production. The reality of their hunger is completely occluded by the representations they fashion; the figure takes over, and constructs a language in which they have no place except as the unrepresented makers of the coins. Commodities (among which, of course, cotton goods were prominent at the time, and hence clothes) exist as means of storing the labor which went into them, which can itself then be efficiently forgotten. It is on the commodity that wealth and exchange are based.

This is a similar intuition about the misrepresentational relation of signifier and signified to that behind Wordsworth's specification of the evils of much of the poetry that he read:

Words are too awful an instrument for good and evil to be trifled with: they hold above all other external powers a dominion over thoughts. If words be not (recurring to a metaphor before used) an incarnation of the thought but only a clothing for it, then surely will they prove an ill gift; such a one as those poisoned vestments, read of in the stories of superstitious times, which had the power to consume and to alienate from his right mind the victim who put them on.

(Prose Works 2. 84–85)

Poisoned vestments indeed. Teufelsdröckh is alarmingly clear about the symptoms and consequences of such alienation and consumption:

Have I not myself known five-hundred living soldiers sabred into crows'-meat for a piece of glazed cotton, which they called their Flag; which, had you sold it at any market-cross, would not have brought above three groschen? Did not the whole Hungarian Nation rise, like some tumultous moon-stirred Atlantic, when Kaiser Joseph pocketed their Iron Crown; an implement, as was sagaciously observed, in size and commercial value little differing from a horse-shoe?

(P. 177)

The flag represents the people, and for its preservation the people themselves are prepared to die; similarly, Kaiser Joseph has really stolen nothing except a device of representation which could be conveniently replaced by any other with no real loss of efficiency. These situations can be read in terms of the anatomy of fetishism; the human mind has abdicated its responsibilities for renovation and recreation by falling prostrate before a particular product of a former creation. As with Godwin's account of the functions of the mace in the House of Lords, the removal or disestablishing of the figure threatens to remind its users that they stand to each other in no properly accountable human relation; naturally dynamic and subversive interests and desires are responsible for the creation of the fetish, and by its means they seek to invest themselves with a false permanence and a material objectivity. All too easily, they succeed.

Dickens's world is not much peopled with flags, crowns, or maces, which do not have much of a place in the daily doings of the middle classes. It is, nevertheless, a tailorized world, as often on the inside as on the outside. One of the earliest novels, *Oliver Twist* (1837–39), echoes exactly the insights of *Sartor Resartus* in this respect:

> There are some promotions in life, which, independent of the more substantial rewards they offer, acquire peculiar value and dignity from the coats and waistcoats connected with them. A field-marshal has his uniform; a bishop his silk apron; a counsellor his silk gown; a beadle his cocked hat. Strip the bishop of his apron, or the beadle of his hat and lace; what are they? Men. Mere men. [Promote them, raise them to higher and different offices in the state; and divested of their black silk aprons and cocked hats they shall still lack their old dignity and be somewhat shorn of their influence with the multitude.] Dignity, and even holiness too, sometimes, are more questions of coat and waistcoat than some people imagine.[2]

Thus Oliver, obliged to greet Mr. Bumble, "made a bow, which was divided between the beadle on the chair, and the cocked hat on the table" (ch. 2, p. 7).

Carlyle could well have been Dickens's most immediate point of reference for this comic rendering of a child's attempt to negotiate the formal reactions demanded by a fetishized world, but there is a long tradition behind Carlyle. Marshall Berman, in a fine study that pertains directly to this part of my argument, has described the different ways in which eighteenth-century writers presented the relation of nakedness to clothing. Thus, for a conservative writer like Burke, nakedness represented a threat to decency and tradition, clothes being the very things we have invented to remove ourselves from a primitive state and to signal forth our differences of rank and hierarchy, the things society exists to preserve. For a contrary tradition, drawing upon the paradigm of Sparta and contributing to a 'Puritan' ideology of plainness and simplicity, nakedness is precisely that condition in which man stands forth relieved of those garments that both operate negatively upon his health and vigor and image a fallen moral condition. Berman identifies an important source (for the eighteenth century) for this latter position in Montesquieu's *Persian Letters*, and it recurs frequently.[3] Here is another formulation from Rousseau's *Discourse on the Moral Effect of the Arts and Sciences* (1750):

> External ornaments are no less foreign to virtue, which is the strength and activity of the mind. The honest man is an athlete, who loves to wrestle stark

naked; he scorns all those vile trappings, which prevent the exertion of his strength, and were, for the most part, invented only to conceal some deformity.

Before art had moulded our behaviour, and taught our passions to speak an artificial language, our morals were rude but natural; and the different ways in which we behaved proclaimed at the first glance the difference of our dispositions.

(*"The Social Contract" and "Discourses,"* pp. 121–22)

The image of honesty is nakedness, and nakedness and honesty are *strong*. In such a state there was a condition of correspondence between outer and inner, appearance and essence, sign and meaning. The passions, Wordsworth might have added, spoke forth in a spontaneous and unrefracted way. Conversely, Rousseau goes on, "there prevails in modern manners a servile and deceptive conformity; so that one would think every mind had been cast in the same mould" (p. 122). The clothing of the body results from and stimulates a recourse to deceit which corrupts both self and others. We image ourselves not as we are but as we are made to be, or want to be. John Gordon saw around him "a set of finical made-up animals, so fond of the little attainments they are masters of, as to despise all natural simplicity" (*Occasional Thoughts*, p. 43). In his many uses of the word *fetish* and its compounds, John Atkins had applied it not only to the cult objects of the natives of Guinea, but also to their personal decorations, and this on the apparent authority of the natives' own usages:

The word *Fetish* is used in a double Signification among the *Negroes*: It is applied to Dress and Ornament, and to something reverenced as a Deity (a Lake, a Stone, a Tree &c.) both so far agree, as to be regarded as a Charm. That by a Peculiarity, and this by some inherent Essence, can *attract Good, or divert Evil.*
(*Voyage*, p. 79n.)

He implies that they in some sense recognized by this double usage the identical ambition in personal decoration and religious persuasion.

The paganized sons and daughters of civilization who tenant Dickens's novels were often not so fortunate or so insightful. His is indeed a world where, whether for reasons of vested interest or unconscious incapacity, "in the great social Exhibition, accessories are often accepted in lieu of the internal character."[4] Fixation upon accessories corresponds to the isolation of certain, single aspects of the human personality as constitutive of identity. This is the source of a great deal of comedy in Dickens, but it is a complicated laugh, and of course in the cases of the villains of society we do not laugh at all:

Was Mr. Dombey's master-vice, that ruled him so inexorably, an unnatural characteristic? It might be worth while, sometimes, to inquire what Nature is, and how men work to change her, and whether, in the enforced distortions so produced, it is not natural to be unnatural. Coop any son or daughter of our mighty mother within narrow range, and bind the prisoner to one idea, and foster it by servile worship of it on the part of the few timid or designing people standing round, and what is Nature to the willing captive who has never risen up upon the wings of a free mind—drooping and useless soon—to see her in her comprehensive truth![5]

That comprehensiveness, we take it, would incorporate a polymorphous variety of human faculties and preoccupations, producing a concept of the "natural" not dissimilar to that held as an ideal by the Romantics. In Dombey's world, such a situation would register as "unnatural." With precise insight into the functions of the inhibited imagination, Dickens makes Dombey himself, like those he conspires to imprison, a "willing captive," in that no alternative is offered him; the mind and spirit will be active, even if in the cause of self-repression, and especially when forms of self-interest accrue. Dombey's acolytes are both the "timid" and the "designing"; those who are not able to challenge the figures of his power, or those who choose not to do so because they see a use for it themselves. Dombey's "master-vice" is but one version of the widespread social concentration of imaginative activity and practical behavior upon inessentials, upon fetishes.

IDOLS OF THE MARKET

In mentioning idols formed by "the reciprocal intercourse and society of man with man" (*Novum Organum* 1. xliii) Bacon seems to have had language principally in mind. But the phrase, at least in translation, conveniently evokes a wider range of forms of "commerce," that which my first chapter has tried to suggest as behind the urgent inquiry into the fetishized imagination in the nineteenth century.

In Dickens's novels these modes of commerce and exchange enacted through fetishized representations are for the most part located in the city. Manipulated contrasts do appear, for example Wemmick's castle and the Peggotty residence on the east coast, but the dominant context is obviously that of the metropolis. Once again, Dickens is drawing upon a tradition here in his perceptions of the dangerous influences on an outsized urban environment. Wordsworth too had drawn upon it in the London episodes of *The Prelude*, even as he admitted to the appeal of the city for the youthful imagination. This tradition has been recently documented by Max Byrd,[6] and Berman also touches upon it in plotting the shift from the image of the city in the *Persian Letters*, where it is a libertarian environment dissolving social ranks and increasing the urge for toleration and self-expression, to that in Rousseau, for whom Paris has become a place of alienation and repression (*The Politics of Authenticity*, pp. 45–53, 113–19). Part of this shift in focus had to do with the size of the city and the amount of commercial and proto-industrial development it was felt to have undergone during the eighteenth century. John Brown thought of the city as corrupting manners by encouraging luxury, gambling, and indulgence (1. 35f.), and analyzed its relation to the country in a way that directly anticipates Wordsworth's fears of tourism reaching the Lakes. Speaking of the fashionable man, he says:

> The Metropolis growing thin as the Spring advances, the same Rage of Pleasure, Dress, Equipage, and Dissipation, which in Winter had chained him to the Town, now drives him to the Country. For as a vain and empty Mind can never give Entertainment to itself; so, to avoid the Taedium of Solitude and Self-Converse, *Parties* of Pleasure are again formed; the same Effeminacies, under new Appearances, are acted over again, are become the *Business* of the Season.
>
> (*An Estimate* 1. 50)

This is the sort of impropriety that Fanny Price senses in the theatricals of *Mansfield Park*. Smollett's *Humphry Clinker* (1771) contains several related polemics, in the voice of Matthew Bramble, against the city and all that it contains. London is a "misshapen and monstrous capital, without head or tail, members or proportion."[7] Its inhabitants are distinguished by their "languid, sallow looks" (p. 120), and among them all social bonds have been dissolved: "Your tradesmen are without conscience, your friends without affection, and your dependents without fidelity" (p. 123). The person who commits himself to London "is hurried about in a perpetual tumult, amidst a mob of beings pleased with rattles, baubles, and gewgaws, so void of sense and distinction, that even the most acute philosophy would find it a very hard task to discover for what wise purpose of providence they were created" (pp. 289–90).

Such are the precedents behind Dickens's representation of the fetishized world of the metropolis, where the clothes-screens have their living and being. Being "nothing but figure," Dickens's characterization operates by the selection of one part or attribute as standing for the whole. Thus firemen are "helmets" (*BH*, ch. 33, p. 282), and Mrs. Merdle is "the bosom" (*LD* 1 ch. 21, p. 156); and when Tom Gradgrind begins to be on good terms with James Harthouse, he is proud to be acknowledged by "such a waistcoat, . . . such a voice . . . such a pair of whiskers" (*HT* 2. ch. 3, p. 74), for those are the insignia in which he would participate as a man of status and fashion. Of course, this is the source of a great deal of comedy in Dickens, carried on by means of extended metaphors like those of "train oil" Chadband and "battleship" Boythorn in *Bleak House*. Such comedy, however, devolves mostly from those figures in whom we suspect a potential for development beyond their particular part or attribute, or from those whose particular besetting mark is least harmful. Where they are incipiently dangerous, like Tulkinghorn, or incapable of change, like Dombey (for much of the novel), the laughter comes harder. For, at root, the obsession with "figure" in Dickens's writing is to be related either to the strategic concealment of an essential or creative character, or to the mannered disguise of a state of emptiness. The figure comes into being as a sign in a system of social exchange, and subsists even (or most especially) where there is nothing to *be* exchanged. Mrs. Skewton is a case in point:

> Thus they remained for a long hour, without a word, until Mrs. Skewton's maid appeared, according to custom, to prepare her gradually for night. At night, she should have been a skeleton, with dart and hour-glass, rather than a woman, this attendant; for her touch was as the touch of Death. The painted object shrivelled underneath her hand; the form collapsed, the hair dropped off, the arched dark eye-brows changed to scanty tufts of grey; the pale lips shrunk, the skin became cadaverous and loose; an old, worn, yellow, nodding woman, with red eyes, alone remained in Cleopatra's place, huddled up, like a slovenly bundle, in a greasy flannel gown.
>
> (*DS*, ch. 27, p. 381)

Once detailorized, there is nothing left, at least nothing that bears any resemblance to the figure that faces the public. Whether it be the Veneerings with their "high varnish and polish" or the Podsnaps as "Podsnap plate" (*OMF* 1. ch. 2, p. 4; ch. 11, p. 90), there are in Dickens a large number of characters who evidence an abdication or enforced loss of the essential or inward self in favor of outward attributes. These relations are almost never "symbolic" (as Coleridge would have used the term); such an authentic mode of signification is rendered impossible, either by the absence of any authenticity within, or by a desire to keep it hidden and out of harm's way.

Action too is distanced and deferred, enacted at the level of the representational rather than the real. When Mr. Pancks takes his revenge on "the Patriarch" (*LD* 2. ch. 32, pp. 507–8) he cuts off his hair and trims down his hat, in a theatrical destruction of his power, or image of that fall. In this instance, at least, it is as well that the action remains thus 'represented,' given what it obviously intimates; Dickens might be taken to insinuate the necessarily figurative nature of certain kinds of human interaction! On the other hand, Newman Noggs is clearly repressed into self-infliction by the demands of his relation to his employer, a price he must pay to remain the hidden agent of charity that he is. Newman is always described as enacting violent physical gestures upon himself; for example, instead of taking Ralph Nickleby by the nose, he "rubbed his own red nose with a vehemence quite astonishing" (*NN*, ch. 44, p. 354). Similar things begin to happen to Micawber when he takes employment under Uriah Heep in *David Copperfield*. Yet Newman Noggs's recourse proves to be the right one, or at least the politic one, in a world gone awry. Nicholas himself does resort to direct physical confrontation when he is outraged; Squeers, Lenville, and Sir Mulberry Hawk all receive drubbings at his hands. But this does not provide a way for him through the complexities of the plot, which depends on a good deal that is outside his control. Direct physical confrontations, however 'real,' are not enough to cope with the unapparent social ramifications of and influences upon events, in the way that they often seem to be in the prelapsarian world of *Pickwick Papers.*

The presence of a concentration of attributes or obsessive habits is in Dickens's writing often a signal that things are badly wrong, whether within or without, or both. Here is the comment on Bounderby's proposal to Louisa Gradgrind:

> Love was made on these occasions in the form of bracelets; and, on all occasions during the period of betrothal, took a manufacturing aspect. Dresses were made, jewellery was made, cakes and gloves were made, settlements were made, and an extensive assortment of Facts did appropriate honour to the contract.
>
> *(HT* 1. ch. 16, p. 59)

Facts too, of course, are but fetishes, resulting from the attrition of the Romantic ideal of polymorphous perception. Louisa submits to Bounderby as Jane Eyre had refused to submit to Rochester's narcissistic desire to convert her to a fetishized form, a public image of his own wealth and station, the object of a smile "such as a sultan might, in a blissful and fond moment, bestow on a slave his gold and gems had enriched."[8] Louisa gives way to main force, in the absence of any support for doing otherwise, and not possessing Jane Eyre's extraordinary inward resolution. Among the ruling classes in *Hard Times* there are no successfully defiant spirits. The normal mode of relation between them is brilliantly intimated in the account of the emotional fracas between Bounderby and Mrs. Sparsit, a model of indirection and deflection:

> Thus saying, Mrs. Sparsit, with her Roman features like a medal struck to commemorate her scorn of Mr. Bounderby, surveyed him fixedly from head to foot, swept disdainfully past him, and ascended the staircase. Mr. Bounderby closed the door, and stood before the fire; projecting himself after his old explosive manner into his portrait—and into futurity.
>
> (3. ch. 9, p. 163)

The striking of the figure is both self-determined and reciprocal; there is no injustice in Mrs. Sparsit surveying Bounderby "fixedly" since he has himself already taken up that posture. The figure she projects is exactly that which he has himself adopted. This kind of interchange, common enough in Dickens, tends to remain merely comic only when it is enacted within the community of the unredeemable, and where that community is not dominant or capable of exercising a determining influence on the innocent or undeveloped. Bounderby and Sparsit deserve each other, and at this point in the novel their control has been effectively disrupted. Just as often, however, one person's figuring of another enacts a clearly repressive function. Little Dorrit is seen as a "plain domestic little creature" in order that her family shall not have to face up to her as anything other than a mechanical convenience: "This family fiction was the family assertion of itself against her services. Not to make too much of them" (*LD* 1. ch. 20, p. 148). Dombey similarly exercises a repressive influence on the community he governs by his assumption of the figures of self-importance and inhuman authority; like Crusoe's idol, he turns round "in his easy chair, as one piece, and not as a man with limbs and joints" (*DS*, ch. 2, p. 17). This assertion of proprietorship immediately prefigures the renaming of Polly Toodle, the godlike act of redetermination and the 'writing out' of the husband who is also standing before him. In a few days Dombey comes to be "invested in his own person, to her simple thinking, with all the mystery and gloom of his house" (ch. 3, ms. A, p. 25). Polly and Susan Nipper at least are not ruined, although they are forced into peculiar strategies in order to remain in their jobs; and even Dombey is redeemed in the end, although only after doing significant damage. Figures like Mr. Turvey-drop—"the Deportment"—in *Bleak House* are, however, more sinister still:

> He had married a meek little dancing-mistress, with a tolerable connexion (having never in his life before done anything but deport himself), and had worked her to death, or had, at the best, suffered her to work herself to death, to maintain him in those expenses which were indispensable to his position. At once to exhibit his Deportment to the best models, and to keep the best models constantly before himself, he had found it necessary to frequent all public places of fashionable and lounging resort; to be seen at Brighton and elsewhere at fashionable times; and to lead an idle life in the very best clothes. To enable him to do this, the affectionate little dancing-mistress had toiled and laboured, and would have toiled and laboured to that hour, if her strength had lasted so long. For, the mainspring of the story was, that, in spite of the man's absorbing selfishness, his wife (overpowered by his Deportment) had, to the last, believed in him, and had, on her death-bed, in the most moving terms, confided him to their son as one who had an inextinguishable claim upon him, and whom he could never regard with too much pride and deference. The son, inheriting his mother's belief, and having the Deportment always before him, had lived and grown in the same faith, and now, at thirty years of age, worked for his father twelve hours a-day, and looked up to him with veneration on the old imaginary pinnacle.
>
> (*BH*, ch. 14, p. 118)

Turveydrop is one of Carlyle's "clothes-screens." He has ruined his wife because she believes in him, and we assume that she does so at least in part because the figure he has chosen for himself is one endowed with societal value and recognition. His worship of the Prince Regent originates a descending series of fetish worships ending in his own son, appropriately named "Prince," who thus wishfully closes the cycle by beginning it again. His imaginary identity derives support from the imaginary aspiration of the others who see themselves through him, and who have no other focus. The master-slave relation as it appears here is not abstractly reciprocal, with each side suffering to the same degree as the other, but is clearly weighted to Mr. Turveydrop's advantage; he subsists very successfully on his own terms, and very obviously at the expense of others. The masters win, along with the masters' masters. It is essential to the logic of the novel that the child of his son Prince and Caddy Jellyby—another parentally oppressed person—should be a physically blighted child.

As figures are the modes of assertion of the possessors and manipulators, on their imaginary pinnacles, so they are in a different way the recourses of the oppressed and intimidated. Recourse to fiction can be a form of self-maintenance in the face of those alternative fictions which are widely held to constitute the real. "Happy Cottage," the painted facsimile of a country retreat inhabited by the Plornishes, is a case in point, "a little fiction in which Mrs. Plornish unspeakably rejoiced" (*LD* 2. ch. 13, p. 361). Wordsworth died seven years too soon to see the confirmation of his analysis of the urban mind creating on canvas its own "nature." A much more forceful instance is Wemmick's castle, a consciously maintained alternative world: "When I go into the office, I leave the Castle behind me, and when I come into the Castle, I leave the office behind me" (*GE*, ch. 25, p. 120). This is no more partial a figure of habitation than the office itself, wherein no "feelings" are allowed (ch. 51, p. 240); the point is that the two never meet. Miss Havisham's house provides another instance of a limiting construction within which experience is manipulated to fit in with rigid and chosen forms and conventions. The castle is an environment made safe for its small community by keeping out the wider world and the office; Miss Havisham's house is a shrine to arrested motion, seeking to stultify and subjugate whatever external energies might fall within its influence. Both are private worlds, and both are figures. We might well prefer one to the other, given the difference between kindness and cruelty; but the novel suggests no forum within the society it describes for the discussion or resolution of such a choice. There is no prospect of either of these limited, constructed environments undergoing the test of universality; Wemmick's home has no chance to win out over Miss Havisham's as a model for society in general, because that society subsists within a figure of its own, that of the office, from which they are both excluded.

Wemmick and Miss Havisham are but two among the disconnected and disoriginated people that inhabit Dickens's novels: orphans, unrequited lovers, children in search of parents, and so forth. The facts of social life which are often responsible for these disconnections also make it dangerous to go about trying to resolve them without the protection of some sort of disguise or indirection. The good spirits, like Newman Noggs, must work unseen, for the innocent avowal of purpose and identity is counterproductive in a world where whatever threatens vested interest will be punished. Just as false images are the symptom of besetting alienation between the parts of society, and of a drastic misdirecting of imagination, so they are also the strategy that must be adopted if one is to have a chance of survival. For Mr. Tulkinghorn, as for his more positive opposite number, Inspector Bucket, knowledge itself is a commodity, something to be exchanged for reward and favor. *Bleak House* is full of people seeking to preserve or discover secrets; thus "Bleak House" itself must misrepresent its identity—it is in fact the place from which all good things in the novel emanate, and not at all bleak—as its owner operates under the disguise of the name "Jarndyce" (homophonous, at the time, with *jaundice*; though even this intuition of the inverse relation between name and nature need not go unquestioned for the reader who sees, as I myself tend to see, something unsatisfying in the positivity of Bleak House and its owner. Perhaps there is indeed a subtle corruption emanating from it, by which insight we reestablish—if indeed we ever abandoned—the authenticity of the name?).

Bleak House does indeed transcribe the operations of a society that is usurping all the proper functions of language, Bacon's principal idol of the market. In this novel it is the law which is the chief offender, and which has achieved exactly the sort of power that Hegel had seen as a threat. The legal process has become

> the property of a class which makes itself an exclusive clique by the use of a terminology like a foreign tongue to those whose rights are at issue. If this happens, the members of civil society, who depend for their livelihood on their industry, on their own knowledge and will, are kept strangers to the law, not only to those parts of it affecting their most personal and intimate affairs, but also to its substantive and rational basis, the right itself, and the result is that they become the wards, or even in a sense the bondsmen, of the legal profession.[9]

Richard Carstone becomes a slave to the task of trying to learn this foreign language, not seeming to realize that its very foreignness is deliberate, its distance purposefully maintained. Thus he can only wear himself out in the pursuit.

Similarly in Dickens's novels at large, the stability or instability of the *name*, that part of language which denominates qualities or entities, is a familiar touchstone. On the one hand, to name or rename someone may be an act of tyranny; on the other, the adoption of a false name may be self-elected as a means of survival. In *Bleak House*, Captain Hawdon becomes "Nemo" and Jobling becomes "Weevle"; to get a job, he takes on the name of a parasitic insect. In *Our Mutual Friend*, John Harmon (the missing letter y almost converts *harmony* into its opposite) takes on a range of false identities in order to assure himself of a society worth reentering. Other characters have less choice, being named by others. Pip becomes "Handel" on a whim of Herbert Pocket's (*GE*, ch. 22, p. 102), as he is indeed to be the handle through which Herbert will arrive at prosperity. Paul Dombey is named after his father and grandfather, as befits his predestined rôle in the continuation of the house; and Dombey senior perversely renames Polly

Toodle in a freak of power which seems even more alarmingly universal when we hear that Mr. Toodle has named his own son "Biler," in homage to the operative part of the steam engine (*DS*, ch. 2). Amy Dorrit participates in her own reductionist rechristening, "Little" Dorrit, because that is what Arthur Clennam calls her, making that name "dearer" to her "than any other" (*LD* 2. ch. 11, p. 348). The floating "I" that is David Copperfield is variously "Brooks of Sheffield," "Daisy," and "Trotwood," and Jenny Wren, who renames the whole world of *Our Mutual Friend*, is herself "the person of the house" or "the doll's dressmaker" (2. ch. 2, p. 148)—real name Fanny Cleaver! It is often a mark of promise and authenticity in a Dickens novel if a character bears an uncoded name, like Mary Graham in *Martin Chuzzlewit* or Madeline Bray in *Nicholas Nickleby*; we can almost be sure that no potential bride for Nicholas would be called "Bobster" (ch. 40, p. 327). The emblematic names often trouble us, and when they are not disguises serve to alert us to an inflexibility of promise and capacity; thus Richard Carstone in *Bleak House* is named after a soft Norfolk stone, pretty and decorative but of little use for building foundations. Then there are names that are incipiently emblematic, like Tulkinghorn and Silas Wegg, suggesting a significance that cannot quite be grasped.[10] Tulkinghorn's name is a kind of secret, like himself, of whom we see "nothing but his shell" (*BH*, ch. 11, p. 86). Only where the name does not claim attention for its own sake can we be sure that all is well within the person it denotes; otherwise, it suggests that the outward sign has usurped the inner being, which is thus effaced from all acts of valorization and exchange. Readers troubled by the credibility of Esther Summerson (summer sun) can only be further exercised by her suitor Woodcourt (would court), who has Jarndyce (jaundice) do his courting for him. Instead of concerning ourselves with the 'reality' of a figure like Esther, we might pay attention to the things that signal her fictionality, and ponder rather the purposes of that fiction.

At the other extreme from the restrictive or emblematic name there is the difficulty of having an insufficient name, or no name at all. In the opening chapter of *Great Expectations* Pip, whom we have seen becoming Herbert Pocket's handle, recalls his denying himself the full name. In the family tombstones, he is confronted at the very moment of entering consciousness with an alien sign-system founded in death and carved in stone. From it he can derive only a tortured and insubstantial identity. If Paul Dombey suffers from being 'overdetermined' as the son of his father, then Pip's crisis happens at the other end of the scale; the objective component in the achievement of identity, the family presence, is erased. Thus the ungainly twitter of "Philip Pirrip" is reduced to "Pip," as if in willed recognition of the emptiness of the surname for a boy who has no parents. Pip assumes self-conscious universality in the name only parodically; he signals himself to the world as disoriginated. Paul Dombey has all too much family,

Pip too little; for Dickens's intuition about the parent is, I think, fundamentally akin to the Romantic formulation of the mind-world relation. Once again we see the predicament of the middle ground. The 'other' must be there in order to stimulate reflexive consciousness, but it must be open to modification by the imagination in such a way that the companionable forms thus generated never become static and monolithic. Pip is denied this principle of growth in being faced with the ultimate monolith, the tomb, as the signifier of the parents he has never known, and from which he (comically) tries to infer their physical identity. The quest for the constitution or completion of identity is thus doomed from the start, and he ends (*pace* the double ending, whose very doubleness I take to be the point) as he begins, still trying to approach a moment of authentically self-determined beginning. Death may be the end of that quest, as the sign of death was its origin, calling up only the 'false' parent, Magwitch. The novel chronicles the ways in which all tentative or incipient movements toward real relation, all "expectations," are whisked away in the vortices of alien systems outside Pip's control. Death (of the parents, of Magwitch) and ulterior interests are the circumstances that persistently rob him of participation in and control of critical experiences. Estella is 'for others' more than she can be for Pip, and Pip himself is 'for' Magwitch in a way that he cannot confront until it is too late to be properly realized in experience.

The presence of the parent, and in particular the male parent, is often enough a repressive principle in Dickens; *Barnaby Rudge*, for example, contains a set of tyrannical parents and parent-figures in John Willett, John Chester, and Haredale. At the same time, the absence of such figures can be just as disastrous, for Dickens seems to have little confidence in the capacity of completely autonomous energies (like, perhaps, Jane Eyre) to achieve a viable self-determination. (And even Jane Eyre comes into a fortune.) The constant theme of the first part of *David Copperfield* is the recollected struggle for the constitution of personal identity. David, like Pip, appears in the world after the death of his father, and is robbed of the dominant presence that must be encountered and supplanted (it seems) if successful maturation is to occur—a process difficult enough anyway, given the inhibitions and misdirections latent in society. David's memory of infancy is of an experience composed of inchoate object-parts never assembled into singleness:

> The first objects that assume a distinct presence before me, as I look far back, into the blank of my infancy, are my mother with her pretty hair and youthful shape, and Peggotty, with no shape at all, and eyes so dark that they seemed to darken their whole neighbourhood in her face, and cheeks and arms so hard and red that I wondered the birds didn't peck her in preference to apples.
>
> (Ch. 2, p. 8)

Of course, the meditation on the construction of the "I" which forms the narrative thread of the opening chapters—the headings to the first six of which all begin with the word *I*—is itself constructed retrospectively, so that the narrator speaks from within the achieved personality whose absence he remembers:

> I could observe, in little pieces, as it were; but as to making a net of a number of these pieces, and catching anybody in it, that was, as yet, beyond me.
>
> (Ch. 2, p. 13)

Whether he ever does catch anybody in it is a question we are to resolve by making a decision about the status of the "vision" of Agnes which ends the book; and certainly for the whole course of his life before that moment, he is condemned, it seems, to repeat that experience of parts. For David is but one-half of the verb substantive, first person. The other half is provided by his double, Ham Peggotty, or "am"—" 'Here's my Am!' screamed Peggotty, 'growed out of knowledge!' " (ch. 3, p. 17). Ham is the figure who is, both physically and thematically, built for the certitude of action from which David's own career remains strangely distant. As "am" (Peggotty's dialect drops the 'H' and signals the link to 'I') he undergoes actively and in his being the sufferings brought about by the cloudy perceptions of the misguided and misguiding "I" who is David, and who imports Steerforth, another directionless, fatherless force—" 'I wish with all my soul I had been better guided!' " (ch. 22, p. 194)—into the society of action, work, and performance. As pure potential subject relying on the society of Yarmouth beach for its conversion into activity, David is a disastrous presence for the kindly rustics who love him so well. That division is also a social one, as the young gentlemen import the guiding principle for those 'below'; for Steerforth is the complement of the anonymous David, an even more 'potential' subject, or "I," who is even more instrumental in carrying through "am's" ruin. They come together only in death.

In David and in Steerforth "I" and "am" are seriously disjoined, so that the "I" must always look outside itself for completion and satisfaction; Steerforth *plays* at being a sailor, dallying only with the outward signs. Similarly, David's own relation to Steerforth is based on *looks*; it is the clothes-screen with which he longs to be associated, like Tom Gradgrind with the whiskers and waistcoat, and he thus has no eye for the inner person, no perception of the absence of such an entity. With a life that is so much composed of acquaintance with and reliance upon figure, we may well question the nature of that representation of Agnes in the closing paragraphs. We should certainly register its representational ambiguity, even if we do not allow it to spoil our ambitions for narrative resolution.

The dominance of the figure in Dickens, which Henry James so aptly noted, can be taken to signal a world upside down and inside out, badly awry in the processes of signification and exchange which it encourages and recognizes. Detached or distorted figures, often metonyms or obsessively emphasized synecdoches—bosoms, helmets, coats, and waistcoats—are fitting to a society wherein (almost) all authentic relations are inhibited or punished. Aside from the redeeming intelligences who operate as the educative centers to the novels, their societies are energetically miscreative. If we can suggest in Jane Austen and (more precariously) in Charlotte Brontë the paradigm of male energy humanized or directed by female intelligence and sympathy, then Dickens offers by contrast a gallery of male characters who often fail to mediate between the demonic and the impotent. Mr. Carker, Mr. Pecksniff, and most obviously Jonas Chuzzlewit and Bradley Headstone, all fail to conceal the elements of cruelty and sadism, or at least drastic self-abandon, in their sexual natures. In contrast many of the minor males, like Mr. Jellyby and Mr. Pocket, are little more than terrified ornaments of their dinner tables; even Clennam and Tom Pinch are, for large parts of the stories in which they appear, passive before experiences imposed on them from outside.[11]

Against this presentation of maleness, one registers the force and integrity of the female bonding in the novels, which can even seem to usurp the newly founded heterosexual society that we expect to emerge at the end. Ada Clare is always "my darling" to Esther, and the joyful announcement of impending childbirth happens (for the reader) between the two friends rather than between husband and wife (*BH*, ch. 60, pp. 506–7). This registers the more forcefully in view of the relative colorlessness of Carstone and Woodcourt. Again, when Edith searches for a way of expressing her guilt and revulsion at Carker's kiss, she finds it in referring to "the cheek that Florence would have laid her guiltless face against" (*DS*, ch. 54, p. 728). Riah, in order to enter into the society of the redeemers, is feminized by Jenny Wren: he becomes "godmother" (*OMF* 3. ch. 2, p. 277).

In this context of disjoined relations between the sexes, where the prospect of authentic exchange seems to be more open to the females than the males, marriage contracts, or proposals of marriage, are often comical or uncomfortable. Mr. Guppy's legal-financial monologues in *Bleak House* are merely lists of his most proudly held attributes offered as a proposal. The marriages of Wemmick and Miss Skiffins, and of Mr. Bunsby and Mrs. MacStinger, are comic treatments of the difficulties of expression and exchange seen in such individual characters as Flora Casby, John Chivery, and Bradley Headstone. In particular Rosa Dartle, marked with the visible sign of Steerforth's wilful and unpunished violence, is one of the fullest of all Dickens's studies of displaced sexual energy. Hers is a passion that takes possession of her whole figure; she becomes the image of a passion, one which "made itself articulate in her whole figure" (*DC*, ch. 32, p. 286), and which can express itself only outside the social and linguistic contract as beyond the range of conventional signification:

I don't know what it was, in her touch or voice, that made that song the most unearthly I have ever heard in my life, or can imagine. There was something fearful in the reality of it. It was as if it had never been written, or set to music, but sprung out of the passion within her; which found imperfect utterance in the low sounds of her voice, and crouched again when all was still.

(Ch. 29, p. 264)

In the same way, Rosa's attempt to wound Emily falls short of its mark: "The blow, which had no aim, fell upon the air" (ch. 50, p. 438). The lack of aim indicates that the blow is the expression of a drive that has no focus within conventional subject-object relations. Like Bradley Headstone, Rosa is in the grip of an uncontainable passion, in her case one poisoned and distorted by Steerforth's behavior.

The alienation of the sexes can seem even more miscreative when it affects the characters who are to be the residual happy couples, prospective of progress and reorigination. In *Barnaby Rudge* the repressive parents and parent-figures are energetically countered and their ultimate defeat is signalled by a final onset of superfecundity. Joe and Dolly have "more small Joes and small Dollys than could be easily counted," and Edward Chester and Emma Haredale have "a family almost as numerous as Dolly's" (ch. the last, pp. 389, 390). This lack of complication is, however, not entirely the norm in Dickens's writing. Nicholas Nickleby is all too ready to admit defeat as he tells his sister Kate of a vision of a future wherein the younger generation will come for sympathy "to the old bachelor brother and his maiden sister" (*NN*, ch. 61, p. 494). His own energies are not enough to fight through the web of inhibitions and impositions surrounding his ambition for a marriage of love. Esther's marriage to Woodcourt is yet further out of the control of the two lovers, being masterminded by the father-figure Jarndyce and remaining under his control to the point of incurring many a reader's out and out disbelief. Little Dorrit's dutiful concentration on her father is at times invaded by a language stronger than that we might expect: "I shall see my dear love, with the dark cloud cleared away. I shall see him, as my poor mother saw him long ago" (*LD* 1. ch. 35, p. 263). Such language may be to a large degree conventional, but again it remains striking in the context of the situation whereby Clennam has to be *told* of her love for him (2. ch. 27, p. 461). Both the leading males seem to be adrift in a sea of self-regard and introspection which cuts them off from a perception of the outside. Effectively, it is Dorrit who proposes marriage to Clennam (2. ch. 34, p. 516).

Just as emblematic of the unprogressive society whose sign-system and mode of exchange is arrested in the dominance of the fetish is the relation between adults and children. This is habitually one of inversion, or topsy-turvy, where the child is the "monster birth" seen by Wordsworth, "no Child,/But a dwarf Man" (*The Prelude* 5. 292, 294–95), and the adult is in a state of childishness, with or without innocence. The Smallweed family gives birth to "little old men and women," and produces children only among its senior members, as when grandmother "fell (for the first time) into a childish state" (*BH*, ch. 21, p. 176). Judy Smallweed and Charley Neckitt, respectively aged fifteen and thirteen, enact between them an adult-child relationship. Joe Gargery is treated by Pip as "a larger species of child" (*GE*, ch. 2, p. 4), and Little Dorrit, a woman "probably of not less than two-and-twenty . . . might have been passed in the street for little more than half that age" (1. ch. 5, p. 33), and is herself "mother" to the unfortunate Maggie, a child of "about eight-and-twenty" (1. ch. 9, p. 63). Jenny Wren, who is "at the most thirteen" (*OMF* 2. ch. 1, p. 143), is mother to her own father, a tortured wreck of disconnected human attributes and parts, "unnerved and disjointed from head to foot" (2. ch. 2, p. 154). Bella Wilfer directs a great deal of emotional energy towards her father, but his relation to her remains unthreatening by virtue of his being desexualized into a little boy (for which his wife is largely responsible); thus he is always "the Cherub." And so on. Paul Dombey's christening is, in fact as well as in figure, a funeral, for he is born into a context where he will have no chance for growth; and the point in life which most exactly expresses the removal of that opportunity is of course death. To have parents may inhibit growth; but the kind of freedom from inhibiting origins which we might expect to find in the predicament of orphanage or illegitimacy is shown in *Great Expectations* and *David Copperfield* to incur its own problems. Thus Dickens's children seem often to have too much parent or not enough, with little chance of finding the balance of within and without so necessary for the constitution of a positive identity.

So much, then, by way of a brief outline of the ways in which Dickens situates the figurative ingenuity of his writing as the image of a world which is on the largest scale disconnected and alienated. Fetishism in the broadest sense, seen as the fixing of attention on one isolated part or attribute which is removed from the dialectic of reprocessing, growth, and the general reciprocal reconstruction of outer and inner, is typical of that world. Arnold makes much of the suicide of a certain Mr. Smith reported in the newspapers, a man 'hebraised' into neurosis by his fixated concentration on "two grand objects of concern . . . the concern for making money, and the concern for saving our souls" (*Culture and Anarchy*, p. 157). Many of Dickens's figures have in fact just one "master-concern" as "talismanic, isolated and all-sufficient" (p. 158). This ultimately produces self-alienation, whether or not it is ever perceived as such by those who suffer it. Bradley Headstone is described by Charley Hexham as an "ornament" to his profession (*OMF* 2. ch. 15, p. 257). In a sense that Charley presumably does not mean to invoke, he is exactly that. He is committed to a "mechanical" relation to his vocation (2. ch. 1, p. 138), which means that he can never derive from it any authentic self-recognition. He is thus in the strictest sense an attribute or ornament, a signifier of something outside himself to which he has no essential relation, and of which he can never be an organic "symbol." This of course duplicates itself in his relations to others; while he is more than an externally determined character, he shows, as does Rosa Dartle, who is herself an attribute in the Steerforth household, the effects of environmental pressure on a person who is not temperamentally able to escape into the saving mannerisms that produce tics, obsessions, and the material for comedy and release.

People fetishize themselves, and are so fetishized by others. Mrs. Bounderby is quite content to come to view her successful son once a year, and from a distance, as befits all worshippers, never allowing herself to be seen, and never actively engaging with the man who has put himself in the position of the favored object. Tulkinghorn, who is an enemy to all life of the sort that is contained in Esther's being allowed a "narrative," is worshipped only by the living dead, like Volumnia Dedlock, who is herself "persuaded that he must be a Freemason. Is sure that he is at the head of a lodge, and wears short aprons, and is made a perfect Idol of, with candlesticks and trowels" (*BH*, ch. 40, p. 350). Dombey's cruelty to his daughter Florence is motivated by his inability to accept her as a substitute for his dead son, in whom the hopes of the house had been lodged. Paul was in fact a function of his father's narcissism, the focus of a parental self-regard that could never allow him to deviate at all from the figure or image it had created. Paul never quite becomes a true fetish because he threatens not to keep still. But it takes Dickens's omniscient narrative to tell us this. Outwardly Paul seems to conform to his father's desire to make him into a thing that cannot feel, an efficient image of his own aspiration to omnipotence. Dickens details this in a masterly passage:

> They were the strangest pair at such a time that ever firelight shone upon. Mr. Dombey so erect and solemn, gazing at the blaze; his little image, with an old, old, face, peering into the red perspective with the fixed and rapt attention of a sage. Mr. Dombey entertaining complicated worldly schemes and plans; the little image entertaining Heaven knows what wild fancies, half-formed thoughts, and wandering speculations. Mr. Dombey stiff with starch and arrogance; the little image by inheritance, and in unconscious imitation. The two so very much alike, and yet so monstrously contrasted.
>
> (*DS*, ch. 8, p. 93)

Dickens's language here seems to speak for an intuition of the phallicism which had from the start (as I shall discuss) been central to earlier accounts of fetishism. We recall Turveydrop on his "imaginary pinnacle," standing atop his own monstrously imaged body-part, which of course can never be *of* his body. Here, Dombey's aspiration to hold and transfix the child as an image of himself is undercut by the author's insistence on the child's inner restlessness. Paul has the *form* of the father, but there is still a spirit within which is of a different order, not yet fully corrupted. The "little image," whilst it outwardly duplicates the paternal stiffness, is inwardly uncontrollable and thus potentially disruptive of the process of reflection, exactly as all authentically confronted exchange, and in particular sexual exchange, must be for Mr. Dombey. That is why its appearance is always greeted by him with cruelty and repression. Against the father's masterconcern for the maintenance of his own public uprightness, the "little image" threatens polymorphous dispersal of interest and affect, "wild fancies" and "wandering speculations." Paul imitates the form, but his mind has not yet been diverted from what Dickens clearly means us to see as the natural by the habitual presence of that form. It may be Dickens's implicit verdict on the self-perpetuating function of alienated male energy that it is the "little image," the vehicle of promise, who dies, and who has to die in order to relax the father out of his figured position.

Dombey as a principle of uninterrupted stiffness seems implicitly phallic; and it must be stressed that his adoption of such a posture is based on an essential lack of control, on a lack of acceptance of the organic body-part itself, which cannot be governed by reason nor perpetuated in its *imaged* condition. Only the loss of the person through whom this image is reflected and on whom its value is focused (compare, again, Wordsworth's "A slumber did my spirit seal") breaks the spell of Dombey's fixation and reintroduces him to his essential humanity. Change precedes the possibility of real exchange, and rings further changes. Only then is he able to love the female, now appearing in the shape of a granddaughter. So well has the lesson been learned that he cries when he kisses her, and is always imagining, at the promptings of his guilt, grievances when none exist. This behavior is a consequence, although of course a benevolent one, of his earlier error. It is itself a new kind of fetishism. You can't teach an old dog entirely new tricks:

> He hoards her in his heart. He cannot bear to see a cloud upon her face. He cannot bear to sit apart. He fancies that she feels a slight, when there is none. He steals away to look at her, in her sleep.
>
> (*DS*, ch. 62, p. 833)

Obsessive as always, but at least now more charitable. Had Dickens written a sequel, we might expect to find the education of Mr. Dombey carrying on after the conclusion we are offered here.

Significantly, that earlier passage describing Dombey and son sitting by the fireside precedes an eruption of the independence of the "little image," who becomes a "presumptuous atom" as he goes on to question the value and nature of money, and its incapacity to buy back the dead mother or the physical health that he himself lacks. He seeks to read back from the figure of money to the reality behind it; he wants to know what it "is," and what it is "after all" (ch. 8, pp. 93–94). Dombey is floored by this. All the terms of explanation he can find have to do with the existence of money as a medium of pure exchange, "circulating-medium, currency, depreciation of currency, paper, bullion, rates of exchange, value of precious metals in the market, and so forth" (p. 93). There is nothing convincingly substantial for him to refer the boy to, so he finds himself invoking a content that is itself again insubstantial, and having to do with the figure one cuts by means of it: money is that which makes us "powerful and glorious in the eyes of all men" (p. 95). Figure purchases figure, and exchange happens exclusively at the level of signifiers that have no access back to authentic experience. That is the social context, one supposes, for Dombey's implicit compulsion to represent himself as the immanent principle of uprightness which he can never 'be.'

The imagery of phallicism in Dickens's description of Dombey and son by the fireside seems unusual in the precision of vocabulary for which I have argued here. It does relate, however, to a similar vocabulary in *David Copperfield*. This novel is inhabited by Mr. Spenlow, the pompous and function-oriented male given to "emphasizing what he said with his whole body instead of his head, on account of the stiffness of his cravat and spine" (ch. 38, p. 334), and by Mr. Murdstone, who is perhaps the most explicitly drawn of all such figures. We can argue, of course, about the accuracy of David's perceptions, for the novel is an autobiographical construct and as such is open to the Wordsworthian interplay of memory and event, past and present. But this hardly matters since we are not exercised by any formal questions about the differences between things as they are seen by David and as they *might* be seen by a detached third person or reader. We would have to pay attention to this if we wanted to build a case for taking the narrator in bad faith, but as it happens (as we shall see) there is external confirmation for what David sees in Murdstone.

Murdstone is consistently put before us as the apostle and embodiment of "firmness." The external manifestation of this is cruelty, and, like Dombey, though in a much less tortured and hence much more irrecoverable way, he punishes both children and females, the images of softness and flexibility. He is attracted to David's mother because "he could mould her pliant nature into any form he chose" (ch. 4, p. 27). David summarizes his memories thus:

> The creed, as I should state it now, was this. Mr. Murdstone was firm; nobody in his world was to be so firm as Mr. Murdstone; nobody else in his world was to be firm at all, for everybody was to be bent to his firmness. Miss Murdstone was an exception. She might be firm, but only by relationship, and in an inferior and tributary degree.
>
> (Ch. 4, p. 30)

The esemplastic tyrant has tailorized and tyrannized his sister also into tributary firmness, as Dombey his young son, and has further impressed upon her an emblematic masculinity: she has "very heavy eyebrows, nearly meeting over her large nose, as if, being disabled by the wrongs of her sex from wearing whiskers, she had carried them to that account" (ch. 4, p. 29). Her brother is her keeper, and she reflects his figure, by displacement. Her times declare that the only thing to be is male, and she pays tribute to that demand.

This view of Murdstone is confirmed at the end of the novel by the doctor who has attended his death. With a deftness perhaps more typical of Melville than of Dickens, he notes a " 'strong phrenological development of the organ of firmness, in Mr. Murdstone and his sister, sir,' " and also that " 'Mr. Murdstone sets up an image of himself, and calls it the Divine Nature' " (ch. 59, pp. 506, 507). Negative as all this is, we should not omit to notice Aunt Betsy's reported ambition that David should become "firm and self-reliant" (ch. 23, p. 215). As has been said, he might have been happier had he had just enough of the Murdstone in his nature (derived from direct experience of the father) to create form and direction in his experience, without having so much as to cease to be open to the creation of new forms and figures. Dickens's world is one in which that ideal Wordsworthian balance seems almost impossible to achieve.

Dickens's novels then are about the various modes of fetishism which he sees, and they are therefore intensely figurative, inasmuch as they are *about* figure. As such they do not however ironize their own coming into being, their own status as potentially partial representations. An abstract formulation of the situation might run as follows: if I am obliged to see the world figuratively myself, given that there is only a figured seeing, how can I in good faith describe the figures of others as improper? Do we not all share the same epistemological mechanism, our representations thus all equally devoid of finality? Wordsworth solved this dilemma by insisting on the impermanence of all figures, which must be continually reprocessed through the individual imagination as its means of constituting a community, and at the same time its relation to that community. He was thus able to say as it were authoritatively that some figures *are* superior to others; those that are unstable are preferable to those that are fixed. At the same time he could say that firm distinctions can be drawn between the kinds of social context which determine or encourage those figures; thus, between the city and the country.

I take the same results to apply to Dickens, though he does not see any need to go through the conscious analysis of this very question of authority as we find it in Wordsworth or in Blake. Dickens validates the least restrictive modes of perceiving, and they are the ones written in as natural to the human heart before it is redetermined by fixed social relations. As functions of growth, change, and active sympathy they are the forces which could keep fetishism at bay. In order that they shall do so Dickens often has to strain the privileges of fiction to contrive endings so providential as to be seriously open to question. But he does not, in his analysis of fetishism, feel obliged to call overtly into question his own status as a partial observer. That radical questioning of one's own authority so important to earlier Romantic writers does not seem to belong in a context where the degree of incumbent fetishization of the social order is such as to demand for its critical articulation a fully fledged alternative order of the 'natural.' More ambiguously, we could also conjecture that recourse to the natural also offers a ready avenue of relief for the harrowed reader, and therefore a guarantee of Dickens's ongoing popularity and perhaps also a way of avoiding the social revolution that elements of his analysis would otherwise seem to require. Read in this way, what may appear as an indictment in fact becomes a safety valve. This issue must be raised although it is no part of my purpose to try to resolve it here.

Whatever our resolutions, we are left with the core of a moral intention in Dickens, a coherent protest against the figurings of a fetishized imagination, social and individual, each fuelling the other. The whole world is brought into line with a few restrictive images. This lies behind his habit of describing nature and the inanimate world as itself an intentional mind as it were 'consciously' pursuing certain interests and ends, in sympathy with the particular human context. The opening of *Little Dorrit* is a densely figured interlacing of the human and the inanimate, an anthropomorphized environment in which all that is "seen" contributes to the dominant effect of immobility and imprisonment. I give but one example:

> A prison taint was on everything there. The imprisoned air, the imprisoned light, the imprisoned damps, the imprisoned men, were all deteriorated by confinement. As the captive men were faded and haggard, so the iron was rusty, the stone was slimy, the wood was rotten, the air was faint, the light was dim. Like a well, like a vault, like a tomb, the prison had no knowledge of the brightness outside; and would have kept its polluted atmosphere intact, in one of the spice islands of the Indian Ocean.
>
> (1. ch. 1, p. 2)

The construction of the passage is one of analogy which asks to be read as causality ("as . . . so . . ."); it insinuates a causal sequence that is ultimately to be located in the capacity of the human mind to *form* the material context and to impose thereupon a particular variety of perspective-consciousness; this is then reduplicated upon others passively entering its sphere of influence. When Dickens writes "the prison," he thus suggests the achieved conglomerate of humanized matter, which *can* then be said accurately to reflect human qualities. The authority of the narrative is actually to be referred to that of the human aspiration or ambition which has indeed created a world of this kind. This particular ambition, it is said, has been so successfully and completely materialized that it would survive even the assault of a diametrically alternative unstructured nature, that of the Spice Islands. Here is Schopenhauer on the mind's powers to construct the image:

> For willing and aims make it so one-sided, that it sees in things only what refers to these, and all the rest partly disappears, partly enters consciousness in an adulterated form. For example, a traveller who is anxious and in a hurry, will see the Rhine and its banks only as a dash or stroke, and the bridge over it only as a line intersecting that stroke. In the head of the man filled with his own aims, the world appears just as a beautiful landscape does on the plan of a battlefield.[12]

In Dickens, this kind of insight is deployed as an analysis of social interaction rather than as abstract individual perception. Representational forms in Dickens are almost always divisive, shared happily by those who have access to the power they encode (others suffer them helplessly, of course). There is no recourse to theory in Dickens, as there often seems to be in Romanticism, no attempt to ensure by a transcendental maneuver a universality or common ground to human experience. The model of the 'natural' may be taken to promise what such a common ground might be, but it is never offered in any secure isolation from the more familiar and threatening alternatives. Thus the hegemony at any moment of a particular image is the license for the description of intersubjective space as correlative to that image. Thus is the common environment colonized by its controllers, much as Dombey has the power to 'determine' the weather:

> If any sunbeam stole into the room to light the children at their play, it never reached his face. He looked on so fixedly and coldly, that the warm light vanished even from the laughing eyes of little Florence, when, at last, they happened to meet his.
>
> It was a dull, grey, autumn day indeed, and in a minute's pause and silence that took place, the leaves fell sorrowfully.
>
> (DS, ch. 5, p. 58)

We do not need to decide, as third-person observers, whether it is really a grey day outside; because Dombey has the *power* to take the light out of Florence's eyes, there is no reference to an assimilable reality possible for her outside the control of that imposed figure. The falling leaves *are* those of her budding humanity, and femininity.

The efficient ruler of society, whether it be an individual or a special interest or faction, is the possessor of the power to compose images and to impose them upon others as reality. Shelley knew this, and that is why he prescribes continual metaphoric activity as the generative element in history and in culture, as in reading. Only the unpredictable and uncontrollable thwartings of "poetry" can maintain the interplay of rival figures, a power all the more necessary in view of the fact that creative lapses into fixity are required from time to time to create culture. We can see also in Dickens that in a totally monolithic society certain strategies can become radically creative again. The metonym cannot, because it almost always signals the draining away of attention from the inner quality to an outward attribute that may have nothing to do with it; thus it is the trope of fetishism. The metaphor, however, can be creative, because of its greater tendency to remain in the province of the mind; if it does materialize then it tends to do so more often in language than in the world of things.

One of the most uncompromising and successfully consolidated world views ever written up by Dickens is that of *Hard Times*, and he presents it as quite well aware of the threat constituted to it by uncontrolled (unrepressed) metaphoric activity of the kind the "little image" promised in its "wandering speculations." Coketown society and the Gradgrind education are founded in "fact," which is of course itself a fetish, an imposed constraint on the kind of phenomenological variability that might remind individuals of their capacities for creating alternatives. The reward for being in total control, and the means of keeping that control, is the calling of figures "facts." Coketown is the social result of the Murdstone-Dombey principle, which has reduced everything to one significance, one way of being seen. Bitzer, the star schoolboy, is the voice of a world with no syntax. Thus he defines a horse:

> Quadruped. Graminivorous. Forty teeth, namely twenty-four grinders, four eye-teeth, and twelve incisive. Sheds coat in the spring; in marshy countries, sheds hoofs, too.
>
> (1. ch. 2, p. 3)

The horse is a series of attributes or qualities never integrated organically into a living form. Between the parts there is no syntax, nothing to encourage movement, lapse, wandering, play. Integration into a whole would involve an act of mind operating upon the assembled parts. If the Coketown world is to work, children like Bitzer must be discouraged from seeing the whole in the parts; that would introduce them to "symbolic" perception and the idea of living form. They must also be discouraged from indulging in representation, because this involves an act of mind (whatever happens to it afterwards). Thus walls must not be papered with images of horses, nor floors carpeted with images of flowers (1. ch. 2, p. 4). To divorce a representation from its "fact" is to allow the mind to become aware of its own powers and to set it wandering. Gradgrind's children are "models" not only in their behavior but also in their existence as constructed personalities (1. ch. 3, p. 5). Coketown is the rewriting of the world Wordsworth reported in London; difference without identity, and identity without difference. Relational apprehension is rendered redundant here because there is no basis for comparison; the streets are "all very like one another," the people are "equally like one another," and the public buildings are indistinguishable one from another: "The jail might have been the infirmary, the infirmary might have been the jail, the town-hall might have been either, or both, or anything else, for anything that appeared to the contrary in the graces of their construction" (1. ch. 5, p. 12). This erasure of the possibility for comparison is a tactic to prevent the potentially destabilizing reassembly of items into subversively new metaphorical configurations. It seeks to inhibit the challenge of other figures to the reality of those already encoded. Bounderby is indeed " 'not to be got to call a Post a Pump, or a Pump a Post, or either of them a Toothpick' " (1. ch. 16, p. 59), as he proudly tells us. To do so would be to give the game away. It is the circus that intrudes into the town as an extraneous society given to flagrant confusion of the figured and the real, and it appropriately functions as the gathering and preserving place for imagination and authentic relation. In this society, the place of the alternative image is the place of hope.

We can see, then, in this novel, some evidence for a polarization of the two main modes of representing, in the form of a working distinction between metaphor and metonym. Insofar as the latter does not stand in any essential relation to what is signifies—insofar as it signifies, in this sense, itself—it is the figure of alienation. This applies whether it is self-imposed, imposed from without, or both at once, as with (for example) Harthouse's investment in his waistcoat and whiskers. The metaphor, on the other hand, is the figure working for the imaginative redistribution of the relations between things; the figure of potentially alternative world orders. In an environment like Coketown, so heavily determined already, the acceptance of metonymic perception and identity (or, of course, synecdoche, with its emphasis on body parts and object parts) might seem the way of passive acceptance, and the way of metaphor that of revolutionary perception. This schema, however, will do best for *Hard Times*, and the activity of making relations between things need not always be energetic or reconstitutive of more promising figures. It is not so for Arthur Clennam as he allegorizes the landscape, the river, and the Meagles family as in emblematic relation to each other, and to life (*LD* 1. ch. 16), precisely as a mode of reading himself out of authentic connection to any of those things, and thus of course to himself. All representation, in other words, whether we choose to call it metaphor or metonym, is positioned by Dickens in a specific context as at the service of particular interests and dispositions. The figure, metaphor or metonym, does not have an autonomous, generic identity from which we may in a formal way infer its value; it must be assessed in the light of its *use* and the effect on the community of its users. That which creates hope in one place may be used in the service of self-delusion in another.

In discovering companionable forms, or having them imposed from without, the mind always risks self-alienation of the kind described in the paradigm of fetishism. Dickens's answer to this is a faith in the human heart as a fundamentally inclusive and generous faculty wherein the many and the one can coexist in creative and charitable harmony. The heart, if it can only be rediscovered and a place found for it, is implicitly generative of new figures and reeducated communities. Even then, we may take it as a measure of Dickens's pessimism that the harmonious groupings that end some of the novels are themselves small (like Wordsworth's mountain societies) and constituted always by deaths and by critical exclusions. It is not at all clear that Dickens is writing about a universal faculty that all people will share, and it is absolutely clear that not all will experience the power and possibility of expressing it, even if they do have it within them. The young Oliver Twist wakes up in the company of the Maylies:

> The melancholy which had seemed to the sad eyes of the anxious boy to hang, for days past, over every object: beautiful as all were: was dispelled by magic. The dew seemed to sparkle more brightly on the green leaves; the air to rustle among them with a sweeter music; and the sky itself to look more blue and bright. Such is the influence which the condition of our own thoughts exercises, even over the appearance of external objects. Men who look on nature, and their fellow-men, and cry that all is dark and gloomy, are in the right; but the sombre colours are reflections from their own jaundiced eyes and hearts. The real hues are delicate, and need a clearer vision.
>
> (*OT*, ch. 33, p. 226)

Is it really true that perception is only intentional when it presents to us a gloomy world, and not when it sees sun and brightness? However we decide that—and Dickens often indeed locates the 'real' in the warmer motives of the human heart—it nevertheless remains the case that those other perceptions recur, just as do the moods determining them, and the things that cause those moods. It is really only moral faith that decides, and outside such faith we see in Dickens figurings that are the result of particular historical pressures and that are shared often only by subgroups of observers, rather than by society as a whole. For society is not a whole. In the following passage describing David Copperfield's return to England after a long residence abroad, what David sees is not what the waiter sees:

> As I followed the chief waiter with my eyes, I could not help thinking that the garden in which he had gradually blown to be the flower he was, was an arduous place to rise in. It had such a prescriptive, stiff-necked, long-established, solemn, elderly air. I glanced about the room, which had had its sanded floor sanded, no doubt, in exactly the same manner when the chief waiter was a boy—if he ever was a boy, which appeared improbable; and at the shining tables, where I saw myself reflected, in unruffled depths of old mahogany; and at the lamps, without a flaw in their trimming or cleaning; and at the comfortable green curtains, with their pure brass rods, snugly enclosing the boxes; and at the two large coal fires, brightly burning; and at the rows of decanters, burly as if with the consciousness of pipes of expensive old port wine below; and both England, and the law, appeared to me to be very difficult indeed to be taken by storm.
>
> (*DC*, ch. 59, p. 499)

This account of the extinction of potential innocence by the weight of maintained attributes is not a universal observation, but a comment on the condition of England, all the more obviously so to the returned traveler. The subject sees himself reflected in a depth of polished surface; that is the world out of which he must reflexively compose his identity. The metonyms are kept efficient in being kept superficial; they reflect from their surfaces, in substitution for the inward reference or 'reading' which they must not encourage, having nothing behind them. All these surfaces, taken together, all these *things*, "seemed to unite in sternly frowning on the fortunes of Traddles, or on any such daring youth" (p. 500). It is a world where human energy spends itself polishing surfaces to collect the wages for the purchase of coats and waistcoats; nothing but figure.

CHAPTER 3

HERMAN MELVILLE: CHASING THE WHALE

Nor has Nature been all over ransacked by our progenitors, so that no new charms and mysteries remain for this latter generation to find. Far from it. The trillionth part has not yet been said; and all that has been said, but multiplies the avenues to what remains to be said.
Melville, *The Literary World*, August 1850

We remove mountains, and make seas our smooth highway; nothing can resist us. We war with rude Nature; and, by our resistless engines, come off always victorious, and loaded with spoils.
Carlyle, *Signs of the Times*, 1829

Dickens may be described as the analyst of fetishism in the city. He reports on a world of reified imaginations, a whole dismembered into parts seemingly incapable of further restoration. There are exemplary, passionate intelligences to be found, but their eventual success, when it occurs, is more a result of fictional privilege than probability. The Dickens world is a jumble of parts and attributes of exactly the sort foreseen by the earlier theorists of the consequences of divided labor and its influences on mind and society.

Melville and Conrad, who are the subjects of the rest of this book, may be thought of correspondingly as the analysts of fetishism on the high seas and in far-off places. They describe the exportation of the values and customs of that same social configuration so critically addressed by Dickens. It is the imaginations and creative powers of the exporters which are already predetermined by the patterns of seeing and believing which they carry within them, and which are reimposed upon the more innocent—or at least different—world.

Melville, in the epigraph to this chapter, speaks of the New World—in particular, as it happens, of Vermont, and of the prospects open to the American writer. What makes *Moby-Dick* a book arguably paradoxical in its message is exactly this New World faith in an environment yet unspoiled, and perhaps vast enough to remain forever unspoilable. The white whale is never caught, and thus the energies that go into pursuing him can be at least partly redeemed, if only by complexity, as being somewhere between positive and negative, demonic and creative. The figures of power and conquest are never final: the world fights back, and its horizons recede. The depths of the Pacific may provide the image of infinity which its eastern shores no longer fulfil with conviction.

Carlyle, conversely, speaks from the Old World, the world that Dickens was about to write. These "spoils" too are ambiguous, but the ambiguity does not force use into contradictory positions. They are riches and rewards, and also acts of transgression, spoilings. The one sense taints the other, and suggests that the gains are ill-gotten, bought at the price of criminal interference. Here there is no sense of charm or mystery; here, "nothing can resist us."

Somewhere between these two positions I shall be suggesting a reading of Conrad, one verging (by fact of residence, perhaps, or time) towards the Old World verdict, with only Marlow and others tugging us back to a world of positive images and an imaginative proliferation of generous principles.

But Conrad and Melville, though coming from different worlds, do have things in common. They both show, as I have said, the idols of the market being carried forth to the societies from whom the very vocabulary of fetishism and idolatry had in the first place been at least partly derived. Such idols have, needless to say, become much more destructive and pervasive than they had ever been in primitive societies. They are no longer as open to idiosyncratic manipulation, to be used or ignored at whim and destroyed if found to be inefficient. They have become solidified, more outwardly fixed and more inwardly infectious, governing now the unconscious processes of the human imagination at the very deepest levels.

In *Typee* Melville makes much play upon the effects of a tailorized invasion on the islanders of the South Seas. He tells the tale of a missionary's wife who inspired nothing less than "idolatry" until the natives realized that she was a mere woman. At this point she was "stripped of her garments, and given to understand that she could no longer carry on her deceits with impunity" (ch. 1, pp. 6–7). In the absurd trappings of the French admiral, Melville sees "the result of long centuries of progressive civilization and refinement, which have gradually converted the mere creature into the semblance of all that is elevated and grand" (ch. 4, p. 29). Typee conversely has no money and no artifice. In a voice echoing that found in Rousseau and other eighteenth-century writers, Melville compares the islanders' nakedness with the habits of his own civilization: "Stripped of the cunning artifices of the tailor, and standing forth in the garb of Eden,—what a sorry set of round-shouldered, spindle-shanked, crane-necked varlets would civilized men appear! Stuffed calves, padded breasts, and scientifically cut pantaloons would then avail them nothing, and the effect would be truly deplorable" (ch. 25, p. 181). *Typee* is eloquent on the way in which insidious forms of civilized fetishism are replacing the primitive flexibilities of paradisal life. As a result of encouraging mindless vanity and the worship of ornament among the locals, and setting up a money system to fuel them, the civilized nations are introducing a mirror image of their own social divisions:

> The chiefs swagger about in gold lace and broadcloth, while the great mass of the common people are nearly as primitive in their appearance as in the days of Cook. In the progress of events at these islands, the two classes are receding from each other: the chiefs are daily becoming more luxurious and extravagant in

their style of living, and the common people more and more destitute of the necessaries and decencies of life. But the end to which both will arrive at last will be the same: the one are fast destroying themselves by sensual indulgences, and the other are fast *being* destroyed by a complication of disorders, and the want of wholesome food. The resources of the domineering chiefs are wrung from the starving serfs, and every additional bauble with which they bedeck themselves is purchased by the sufferings of their bondsmen; so that the measure of gew-gaw refinement attained by the chiefs is only an index to the actual state of degradation in which the greater portion of the population lie grovelling.
(Ch. 26, pp. 188–89n.)

But at the same time as all this is accurately enough moralized by the narrator, in the tradition of so many eighteenth-century writers who had pointed out the mechanisms and dangers of a 'refined' society, there is yet a significant taint of self-implication in his account. Exposed to an alternative culture, he certainly does not go in for the burning of idols, as Crusoe did. But he does partake of another version of the Puritan inheritance. Besides being a prisoner in the valley (the natives rightly fearing the incursion of more of his kind) he also seems spontaneously dissatisfied: "I can scarcely understand how it was that, in the midst of so many consolatory circumstances, my mind should still have been consumed by the most dismal forebodings, and have remained a prey to the profoundest melancholy" (ch. 16, p. 118). Though he can see the case for preferring Typee over what he has been born into, 'paradise' is yet dissatisfying. Not being a middle ground between hell and heaven, there is nothing for the strenuous consciousness to *do*; play and pleasure themselves become stale for lack of contrast. As, in Dickens, we may infer that the child with no father faces problems just as serious as the child crippled by the imposition of monolithic authority; or, in Hegel, that the paradigm demanded by Hebrew theology is unworkable in its insistence on a totality that is everything and therefore nothing; so, here, the civilized mind becomes frustrated for lack of a focus, an 'other' through which it may anxiously identify itself through reflection. Because he is not to be allowed to escape, he is constantly watched: "not for one single moment that I can recall to mind was I ever permitted to be alone" (ch. 17, p. 124). If isolation and alienation are the curses incumbent upon man after the Fall, and companionship conversely a prelapsarian ideal, nevertheless that ideal can become unbearable, as it does here, for lack of alternatives. It would be too weighty a reading to suggest that the narrator is passionate in his pursuit of the alienation to which his social and theological training have already habituated him, but we are at least to register the presence of a compulsion that reappears much magnified in *Moby-Dick*.

For the moment, however, I wish to explore another pattern in *Moby-Dick*. For Melville and Conrad also share, being seamen both, an interest in the symptoms and effects of the autonomous male imagination. In the world they write about, male energies are the determining forces, and male figures their images and signs of exchange. Melville hardly writes about women at all, and in Conrad's novels of the colonial experience—which are the ones I mean to discuss—women typically remain tragically unfulfilled, prophetic of an emotional and social order that has no place in the world already figured. The analysis of the figurative mode that is to be accounted for in Melville and Conrad seems to insist more firmly than ever on the forms of the male psyche as the essential components of the available reality. Fetishism and idolatry, worship of things and of fixed images of the human in their various combinations, seem again to emerge more forcefully than before as founded in the subjective aspirations implicated in phallicism and narcissism. The cycle of desire can now be located, in Melville particularly, as part of a psychology belonging to the male subject and its search for a (specifically) sexual identity, which now becomes both the source and the reference of the fetishistic operation.

Phallicism, defined in terms of its 'rhetorical' characteristics, is a metonymic activity that seeks to persuade its user and his audience that it is in fact synecdochic. The phallus is *not* the penis, but seeks to confirm that it is. It is therefore a detached emblem that must always signal a lack, or a sense of incompletion, and concentration upon it sets in motion a quest that is by definition impossible to fulfil. As a representation it is always alien, never properly open to conversion into the body-part it seeks to image forth. To attempt to accomplish this conversion, by chasing the whale, is to set going a process that can only end in death, unless there is a genuine reeducation of the content and aspiration of consciousness. Further, the mechanisms of the search are shown to contain within them the sources of the compulsions for commerce and colonial expansion, which themselves now become imaginative activities. Mind and matter, the realm of ideal aspirations and the lust for profit, are now inextricably interdetermining, each of the other.

Phallicism, as I have said, is entirely an activity of *representation*; it can never have any place in a direct discourse. Indeed it may be that the very idea of a direct discourse about sexuality and the sexual identity (one which is not, that is to say, performance) is a contradiction in terms. Perhaps any theory of sexual relation and exchange must by definition prescribe its own indirection and fail to encompass the limits of its own deviations, or wanderings. I shall try to show that phallicism, at whatever level of conscious or unconscious decision, is central to the treatment of figures and images, most explicitly in Melville's *Moby-Dick*, but also in Conrad's novels of the colonial experience, where it tends to appear more elliptically.

Phallicism was, in fact, central to the theory of fetishism from its early stages. Dulaure devoted his entire second volume to the subject, deriving its incidence from an original worship of the bull and the he-goat, this giving rise to a spate of derived images of sexual prowess (tree trunks and so forth), including the male organ. From thence, attention passed from part to whole, to the whole human form. Phallicism thus becomes the origin of idolatry, and as such is an original component of all forms of humanized religion. Payne Knight's *An Inquiry into the Symbolical Language of Ancient Art and Mythology* (London, 1818) had also placed strong emphasis on the priapic, and this work remained one of the 'unofficial' source books for the theory of fetishism as it developed through the nineteenth century. For Payne Knight, the universality of priapic images was "acknowledged to the latest periods of heathenism" (p. 14), and he goes so far as to suggest that the "spires and pinnacles, with which our old churches are decorated, came from these ancient symbols" (p. 78). Further, Meiners's *Geschichte der Religionen* has a whole section on phallicism (1.251–67).

Looking back to the incidents from *Robinson Crusoe* and *Typee* discussed in chapter 1, it will be remembered that the idols therein described had implicit if not overt phallic characteristics. James King, the author of the last volume of Cook's *Voyage*, had also remarked that some of the islanders "give a place in their houses to many ludicrous and some obscene idols, like the Priapus of the ancients" (3.160). In the researches of nineteenth-century anthropologists into the subject of fetishism, it is noticeable that the unabashed discussions of phallicism offered by the earlier theorists begin to disappear or undergo tactful transformations. James Fergusson's *Tree and Serpent Worship* (1868) speaks darkly of certain "unhallowed rites,"[1] but says nothing explicit about phallicism. M'Lennan's important articles, which came a year later,[2] move the focus of scientific interest towards totemism and away from fetishism in its looser and broader definitions. Totemism is "fetishism *plus* certain peculiarities"— specificity to a tribe, matrilineal inheritance, and relation to marriage laws (1. pp. 422–23). This totemism, whatever origins it might be thought to have in phallicism (the most famous instance of the totem is the pole), becomes with M'Lennan a tool in the organization of primitive societies along rational lines.

For the anthropologist, description of functions and effects replaces (for the most part) speculation about origins.[3] This is the tradition that Frazer inherits, though he does, notably, address himself to origins in speculating that totemism began out of "an ignorance of the part played by the male in the Generation of offspring" (*Totemism and Exogamy* 4.61). The woman consequently identifies the moment of conception with the first stirrings in the womb, and associates this with whatever is near her at the time, which then becomes a totem. This is quite close to the origin John Atkins had suggested for fetishism (*Voyage*, pp. 79–82). It is, in one way, the obverse of phallicism, in which a clear *consciousness* of the power of the generative organ is what inspires the worship of images related to it.

Perhaps Frazer's theory partakes of something like a 'reflected' innocence, something the Victorians might have liked to believe in as typical of undeveloped humanity. The contrast of this origin model with that of phallicism is interesting in that the two taken together seem to reflect something close to the extreme polarity that characterizes the representations of males in Dickens's novels. Those who are demonic and aggressive may be thought of as analogous to phallus-worshippers, committed to forceful images of themselves. Conversely, the weak and listless compare with those totemists who have no awareness of any potential sexual energy in themselves, who have abdicated any control over procreation. There is nothing redeeming in the contrast, of course, since both extremes are forms of impotence.

Literature, perhaps, could afford to be more explicit than the developing social science of anthropology, perhaps because it is more implicit in the first place, demanding an activity of interpretation rather than offering anything much in the way of propositional statements. The preceding historical and theoretical connections between fetishism (or totemism) and phallicism do, however, seem helpful in identifying the context of, for example, Dickens's analysis of the alienating functions of representation in a fetishized society. This alienation is evident even when the choice of an image is apparently self-elected; self and society are mutually determining. Mr. Turveydrop's figurative residence atop the "imaginary pinnacle" instances an alienation that is all the more horrifying because it is not brought to consciousness by any of those who suffer from it. There is no potential for correction, as there might be with Dombey's "little image," who is capable of inward deviation even as he outwardly reflects the father's posture. Paul Dombey's questions about money fracture the narcissistic aspiration projected by his father. Dombey also seeks to extinguish the presence and identity of the female, another force that threatens the integrity of the image, and he enlists the services of Mr. Carker in this respect. Here too the 'other' emerges in revolt, though it is revolt by reduplication. Having been for so long a dinner-table witness to Dombey's hegemony enacted in the public humiliation of his wife, Carker is denied self-dependence by the 'Murdstone' principle of exclusive firmness. But the tributary firmness eventually fights back, and Edith of course becomes imaginatively enmeshed in his revenge against the master. Truly corrupted, Carker too can only assert himself by displaying his own capacity to humiliate others.

He thereby demonstrates a process already described by Godwin:

> But to be the subject of an individual, of a being with the same form, and the same imperfections as myself; how much must the human mind be degraded, how much must his grandeur and independence be emasculated, before I can learn to think of this with patience, with indifference, nay, as some men do, with pride and exultation? Such is the idol that monarchy worships, in lieu of the

divinity of truth, and the sacred obligation of public good. . . . May we bend
the knee before the shrine of vanity and folly without injury? Far otherwise.
Mind had its beginning in sensation, and it depends upon words and symbols
for the progress of its associations. The truly good man must not only have a
heart resolved, but a front erect. We cannot practise abjection, hypocrisy and
meanness, without becoming degraded in other men's eyes and in our own.

(*Enquiry* 2.77)

The emasculation, the unmanning of the "front erect," takes place by the
transference of the image of firmness to another human being, the king. As
that which now excites worship, the king becomes the essential self of the
worshipper. The truly independent man must have not just the inward
identity of self-subsistence, the "heart resolved," but also the outward image, the "front erect." Because the mind grows by words and symbols, he
must maintain the *image* within his control, lest he subsequently lose the
inward condition that that image speaks forth. It is not possible, within
this idea of the mind, to retain the one without the other. The standard
quietism, which recommends the ignoring of outward, worldly relations
and signs for the sake of authenticity within, is here discounted. We cannot
ignore the demands of kings and priests, nor displace them as having
merely superficial implications. There is a direct reciprocity between surface and content, as there was, implicitly, for Wordsworth in his retrospec-
tive analysis of the effects of carrying the surplice, the badge of belonging.
Godwin's language here suggests that sexual dominance and passivity are
implicated in the master-slave relationship and the forms of imaginary
relation which it generates.[4]

I now pass on to *Moby-Dick*. To say that the novel is about the male
imagination is to say nothing new; and, insofar as it is also about phallicism, one can only marvel at the directness of the indirection.[5] The quest of
the *Pequod* is a quest for completion, for the capture of what is lacking,
and it incorporates within the sphere of its ambitions everything from
abstract knowledge of the most apparently dispassionate sort to commercial prosperity and the urge for gain. The various levels of the quest inter-
act and even conflict with each other, and there is no sure way of keeping
them apart, either in fact or in theory. We must never forget, also—as I
shall often perhaps seem to forget for the purposes of this exposition—that
Ahab, however demonic and outrageous his behavior might seem, has
already, as a matter of fact, before the story begins, been robbed of his leg,
and probably of something else besides, by the white whale. If the figuring
mind takes twists and turns beyond what we might think of as the normal,
then we should not forget the rationale that Melville has written into the
factual elements of Ahab's past. What may be more open to question, I
think, is the nature of the appeal Ahab extends to the crew, and to Ishmael.
For this is a world of idols, in which all characters move and have their

being. Queequeg's idol is an obvious idol, but whales are idols too, analogues of human self-completion. Thus Ishmael meditates at the masthead:

> There you stand, a hundred feet above the silent decks, striding along the deep, as if the masts were gigantic stilts, while beneath you and between your legs, as it were, swim the hugest monsters of the sea, even as ships once sailed between the boots of the famous Colossus at old Rhodes.
>
> (Ch. 35, p. 252)

He inscribes himself into a position of absolute power, with all created things "beneath" as attributes of his identity; but the image is perfectly balanced, for it implies both control over what is swimming between the legs (possession), and also terror, fear of losing what is already possessed to other, free floating, forms. Melville here conveys the dialectic of mastery and slavery at a single stroke, and it is resolved for Ishmael by inactivity and repetition. The phantasized omnipotence of life at the masthead is offset by the physical discomfort of being there—"so sadly destitute of anything approaching a cosy inhabitiveness" (p. 253)—as well as by the inverse intuition of having *nothing* under the feet, between the legs. The superimposition of everything and nothing produces a "languor" and a suspension of discriminating consciousness which leads to the calenture, a description of which, along with the death wish implicit in it, ends this chapter, as a warning to the aspiring Pantheist not to depart from the sense of distinct identity. This separate self may indeed impose an anguish of individuality (which Ishmael seeks to overcome in bonding with the society of the ship) and its public dimension, a personalized misreading of the world; but, it is suggested, it is all we have if we are to remain alive. Consciousness is a fact, to be cancelled only by the fact of death.

Of all the forms that float between Ishmael's legs, the white whale is the most overburdened with human aspirations and self-images. Indeed, it is crucial that Moby-Dick, who has already been set apart by being named— "Sir sailor, but do whales have christenings?" (ch. 54, p. 362)—is *not* completely white. The white patch upon his brow is made to represent and mythologize him as white; the part is made to stand for the whole. He too is worked upon by this compulsive habit of alienated humanity, by being imaged into a form that distinguishes him most efficiently from other whales, and heightens his emblematic potential as a receiver of human readings. The actual, observed features of the whale are only partially, emblematically, white. He has "a peculiar snow-white wrinkled forehead, and a high, pyramidical white hump." These are his "prominent features," the "tokens whereby . . . he revealed his identity." The rest of his body is indeed "streaked, and spotted, and marbled with the same shrouded hue" (ch. 41, p. 281), but it is the parts that Melville chooses to stress, in a way that distances his account from that in the sources he apparently drew upon, wherein the whale is described as "of the purest, most brilliant white" (p. 987), or, in another instance, *"white as wool!"* (p. 993). It is the taking of part for whole that we are to register, entangled as it is in the mesh of rumors and metaphysical speculations that make up the chapter devoted to Moby-Dick (ch. 41).

As Moby-Dick in particular, so whales in general are objects for figuring. The very name of the species, the "sperm whale," is "philologically considered . . . absurd." The name had its origin in the idea that "this same spermaceti was that quickening humor of the Greenland Whale which the first syllable of the word literally expresses." When this myth was exposed, the "original name was still retained by the dealers; no doubt to enhance its value by a notion so strangely significant of its scarcity" (ch. 32, p. 232). The poor beast is, it seems, doomed from the start as the focus of the most grandiose phantasies of potency, cunningly maintained as they are by those earning a living from its exploitation.[6] Attempting to replace this mythology by something more scientific, Ishmael is obliged to give up the task of taxonomized parts, "detached bodily distinctions" (p. 234), in favor of a simple division by size. The true whale is unavailable, except in "volume" (p. 235), and thus exists as the sounding board for the genesis of an imaginary science, one that casts its findings in the most desired terms of companionship. It is the head of the whale which contains the precious oil, casing it within an "enormous boneless mass" of a toughness "inestimable by any man who has not handled it." This head has an "unobstructed elasticity" because it is "susceptible to atmospheric distension and contraction," and it is directed by the "mass of tremendous life" behind it. Thus the whale's "concentrations of potency," and the "irresistibleness of that might" (ch. 76, pp. 444–45), are teasingly imaged forth as parts having not a bone in them.

The whale is an "expansive monster" (p. 445) indeed. In the discussion of "The Nut" (ch. 80), Ishmael tries to answer his own question;

> How may unlettered Ishmael hope to read the awful Chaldee of the Sperm Whale's brow? I but put that brow before you. Read it if you can.
> (Ch. 79, p. 455)

Put it before us he does; "phrenologically" speaking, the head is "an entire delusion," and the whale "wears a false brow to the common world" (ch. 80, p. 456). For the brain is very small, hidden away inside the skull, not represented on the surface. Ishmael, correspondingly, seeks to emphasize "the wonderful comparative magnitude of his spinal cord" as a measure of identity. For this *is* represented, by the hump, the proper emblem of the firm column that makes up the whale's personality: "From its relative situation then, I should call this high hump the organ of firmness or indomitableness in the Sperm Whale" (p. 457). This reading of the whale is of course a representation, and one that seems to function at the service of specific interests. The murdering by dissection reconstructs the whale as an efficient image of the phallus. The hump is always firm and always *seen* to be firm; the other "organ of firmness" is neither. Thus the ship's carpenter, "manmaker," refashioning Ahab's stiff leg, adverts to the refiguring of the human form which both sets in motion the quest and is further modified by it: "That is hard which should be soft, and that is soft which should be hard" (ch. 108, p. 580). And Ahab, bitterly exercised by the mixture of recollected sensation and actual absence, threatens to order "a complete man after a desirable pattern" (p. 581).

Moby-Dick, however, who is more beautiful than "the white bull Jupiter" (ch. 133, p. 656), does not subscribe to defeat, and he therefore remains to illuminate the pattern of desire that fuels the quest. That desire is necessarily only a desire for the *image*, at least as far as Ahab is concerned, and this in turn is only represented by substitution, as we have seen. For most of the time Moby-Dick withholds "from sight the full terrors of his submerged trunk" (p. 657), refusing to accede to the demand for full exposure, 'utterance,' and the control of the image (if *only* the image) which might be satisfied by revelation. He taunts Ahab, indeed, with this refusal to reveal, and does so again in the "pitchpoling" phenomenon that occurs when Moby-Dick has Ahab absolutely at his mercy:

> vertically thrusting his oblong white head up and down in the billows; and at the same time slowly revolving his whole spindled body; so that when his vast wrinkled forehead rose—some twenty or more feet out of the water—the now rising swells, with all their confluent waves, dazzlingly broke against it.
>
> (P. 659)

This is also a grotesque and acquiescent parody of what Ahab cannot do; for Moby-Dick, as well as condemning Ahab to that unnaturally hard ivory leg, has probably robbed him of another unmentioned member:

> all loveliness is anguish to me, since I can ne'er enjoy. Gifted with the high perception, I lack the low, enjoying power; damned, most subtly and most malignantly! damned in the midst of Paradise!
>
> (Ch. 37, p. 266)

Harold Beaver has pointed out (p. 729) that Queequeg's overtly phallic idol, Yojo, is named as a palindrome of "O joy." Ahab's inability to experience joy, which is what the whale perpetuates in refusing (or so it seems) to kill him off when it first has the chance, condemns him to an unending quest for substitutes. The ship's carpenter speaks again:

> "Seems to me some sort of Equator cuts yon old man, too, right in his middle. He's always under the Line—fiery hot, I tell ye!"
>
> (Ch. 127, p. 636)

The devil's all below; but only by substitution, by proxy, through a companionable form. The paradoxical identity of Moby-Dick consists in the doubling of motives whereby he is both the object on whom revenge must be taken and at the same time the image of the lost member which must be conquered and regained. Outer form and inner impulse, cause and effect, are in conjunction here, and as so often in this book we cannot be sure that Melville means to encourage any simple criticism or moral animus against the incomplete Ahab. Whatever compulsions he obeys in figuring the whale, there seems little doubt that it has given him ample motive.

In a peculiar way, Ahab and Moby-Dick are doubles; at least they are so figured by Ishmael. At first sight, Ishmael is appalled by Ahab, just as he will be by the whale. Ahab has a mark on his face which is "lividly whitish," and we are soon told "that for the first few moments I hardly noted that not a little of this overbearing grimness was owing to the barbaric white leg upon which he partly stood" (ch. 28, p. 219). As we shall see, Moby-Dick's whiteness occasions a long disquisition on the horror caused by that color, or absence of color. Ahab comes to identify with the whale, "not only all his bodily woes, but all his intellectual and spiritual exasperations" (ch. 41, p. 283). The reflexivity implicit in his threat, "I will dismember my dismemberer" (ch. 37, p. 266), is enacted also in the mirror imaging of the body-parts that they project to the outer world. As Moby-Dick shows a "wrinkled brow" (ch. 36, p. 259; ch. 44, p. 301) or "wrinkled forehead" (ch. 41, p. 281) as the sign of his identity, so Ahab too shows a "wrinkled brow, till it almost seemed that while he himself was marking out lines and courses on the wrinkled charts, some invisible pencil was also tracing lines and courses upon the deeply marked chart of his forehead" (ch. 44, p. 298). As his "snow-white new ivory leg" matches the whale's hump, so, when he goes back to the charts, it is again with a "wrinkling" of the brow (ch. 109, p. 585), reading himself thus into an imitative (and thus worshipful) relation to the figure of his pursuit. It is Ahab's "unappeasable brow" (ch. 135, p. 682) that Starbuck sees with his last earthly glance, as he too is mesmerized into the circle of duplication and compulsion, to his death. Thus operates the mirrorlike dialectic of fetishism.

However negatively or positively we read Ahab's relation to the white whale, it is clearly a relation dependent upon substitution and reflection rather than upon achievement and conjunction. This pertains even in death. It is the Parsee, himself always written into an almost magnetic connection with his captain, who dies the death most properly befitting Ahab himself, strapped by the harpoon line to the whale's back, his "half torn body" (ch. 135, p. 679) thus disjunctively connected to the object that his master has in such a tortured way worshipped and hated for so long. Man and whale belong together, but only in a metonymic relationship, held by rope. That is the answer to the assumption of control Ahab seeks in his revenge—so suffer all men wedded to their tools—and it is itself presented *to* him rather than enacted *by* him. Ahab is thus made to see, at a distance, his own predicament of distance *imaged* in the Parsee. For Ahab himself dies in utter silence, strangled and dragged from the boat, though not before he has commented on the final disjunction or distance forced upon him, dying away from his ship, "cut off from the last fond pride of meanest shipwrecked captains" (p. 684). Always cut off.

This is indeed a book about substitution on the grandest scale, and not just in the personalized context of Ahab's quest. Just as the collected etymologies and the various data which preface the story do not encapsulate the whale, so none among the activities of deflection and representation taking place in the narrative ever manages to produce that apparently sought-for "full utterance"—the phrase is Conrad's, as we shall see. Ahab tries to integrate Moby-Dick into the most familiar and apparently manageable form of social exchange and shared meanings, the money system, in offering the doubloon as the reward for the first sighting. But this gesture is at once undermined by the 'mad' discourse of the ship's boy, Pip, as he sees it nailed to the mast:

> "Here's the ship's navel, this doubloon here, and they are all on fire to unscrew it. But, unscrew your navel, and what's the consequence? Then again, if it stays here, that is ugly, too, for when aught's nailed to the mast it's a sign that things grow desperate. Ha, ha! old Ahab! the White Whale; he'll nail ye!"
>
> (ch. 99, p. 546)

Reference to the old joke, of which most editors remind us (but which in fact invites reference to the falling off of more than one body-part), highlights the prospect of loss within the sign which asks to be taken as gain. The sighting of the whale thus threatens the dismembering of the ship and of all who sail in her. But the ship is already committed to disaster, by the fact of the nailing to the mast, the concentration of energy into a single, obsessive direction. And the doubloon is in fact not at all a principle of exchange but yet another example of Ahab redoubling himself. No other sailor manages to anticipate him in spotting the white whale, so that the reward he has offered in fact devolves on himself: "No, the doubloon is mine, Fate reserved the doubloon for me. *I* only; none of ye could have raised the White Whale first" (ch. 133, p. 655). The coin is his image, the thing that purports to be outside him, but that is in fact within in its essential purposes. Thus, when he fixed his "riveted glance" on the "riveted gold coin," he too "wore the same aspect of nailed firmness" (ch. 99, p. 540). Within is without, for Ahab.

That the crew accept and respond to this challenge may speak for their complicity, reluctant or otherwise, in Ahab's quest. There is a way, indeed, in which their very presence on the ship suggests an acceptance of the cycle of substitution on which that quest is based. Ishmael and Queequeg began by being wedded, figuratively, as a "cosy, loving pair" (ch. 10, p. 148), and that wedding is a microcosm of the society of the ship as a whole. Whatever level of self-election might have been involved at the start of the voyage, there is no doubt that Ahab's despotic captaincy makes it hard for the crew to resist him; at the same time, this is not of itself enough to account for the continuance of the quest. For in revealing the purpose of the voyage to be the single-minded pursuit of the one white whale, Ahab has "directly laid himself open to the unanswerable charge of usurpation," to the point where the crew could "refuse all further obedience to him, and even violently wrest from him the command" (ch. 46, pp. 314–15). Ahab must thus instil into them the same sense of purpose he feels in himself: "your own condescension, *that* shall bend ye to it. I do not order ye; ye will it" (ch. 36, p. 264). Melville may here be suggesting something akin to Godwin's insight into the inwardly eroding function of the outward image of authority. The man who lives under a king cannot be capable of independent decision and cannot but be bent to the purposes of those who rule over him. To resist authority would be to fight against that tendency in himself which approves and identifies with the images of power. Additionally, it may be that the images Ahab does invoke appeal to a common conviction in the crew—all men, after all—so that they identify with the fitness of the quest. Whatever the reason, when the chase is on, the crew of the *Pequod* become as the obedient limbs of Ahab's body, organic substitutes for what he does not have:

> They were one man, not thirty. For as the one ship that held them all; though it was put together of all contrasting things—oak, and maple, and pine wood; iron, and pitch, and hemp—yet all these ran into each other in the one concrete hull, which shot on its way, both balanced and directed by the long central keel; even so, all the individualities of the crew, this man's valor, that man's fear; guilt and guiltiness, all varieties were welded into oneness, and were all directed to that fatal goal which Ahab their one lord and keel did point to.
>
> (Ch. 134, p. 666)

Here the many are reduced to the one, variety to conformity, the polymorphous to the fixated, to the "long central keel" that is the vehicle of Ahab's monomania. Ahab becomes the vehicle of the others' energies, their "keel." The act of irresistible will directs all ulterior motives to itself, and destroys the differences that would offer a basis for doubt or debate. In the case of most of the members of the crew, Melville gives us nothing to allow us to distinguish choice from necessity in their having become whalers; but at this moment, all such questions are redundant.

Even at less active moments, the task of sorting out the outwardly determined from the inwardly (socially or individually) projected seems an impossible one. We have no sure methods for telling apart what is enforced on people by environmental and technological necessity and what is the product of the compulsive urge for companionable form. For example, the investment in images is quite literal for the "mincer," who tailorizes himself into, "slips himself bodily into," the inverted skin of the whale's penis, "that unaccountable cone," the "grandissimus" which was in olden times an idol; at least its "likeness" was (ch. 95, p. 530). The practical and the imaginative are coinstantaneous, impossible to sort into cause and effect. This "cassock" may indeed be the one thing that will "adequately protect" the mincer in his particular job, but it is also a magical-religious "investiture" that is "Immemorial to all his order;" it is an assumption of "canonicals." Technology usurps natural sexual functions in order to exploit nature the more efficiently; it does so by figuratively casting itself as embodied sexuality.

In this way the commercial questing of the whale is enwrapped within a deeper aspiration whose exact limits are never spoken to us. Jest and earnest, cruelty and suffering, man dwarfed by nature or man digesting it to his purposes, these options and extremes are not presented to us in terms of a propositional moral decision. Appropriately, all of Ishmael's meditations on and around whales proceed by analogy rather than by assertive evidence. The object of definition can never be presented or essentialized; it exists rather as a series of infinitely deflected schemas and possibilities. Chapters 55 through 57 are mostly about what the whale is not, a history of the various misrepresentations that have gathered around it. The educated whaleman sees whales everywhere; in the stars, in the mountains, and so forth (pp. 377–78). But these are only "images," whether of a monomaniac preoccupation or a habitual association. Too much whaling makes one see only whales. It is the revenge of divided labor that an alternative reality is ungraspable, or ceases to exist. But it is also in the nature of whales proper that they refuse to be decisively imaged, so that

> you must needs conclude that the great Leviathan is that one creature in the world which must remain unpainted to the last. True, one portrait may hit the mark much nearer than another, but none can hit it with any considerable degree of exactness. So there is no earthly way of finding out precisely what the whale really looks like. And the only mode in which you can derive even a tolerable idea of his living contour, is by going a whaling yourself; but by so doing, you run no small risk of being eternally stove and sunk by him. Wherefore, it seems to me you had best not be too fastidious in your curiosity touching this Leviathan.
>
> (Ch. 55, p. 271)

Even visual contact does not produce such sought-for knowledge, merely a "tolerable idea" of the "contour."

Ishmael's appetite for the companionship of outward images is as compulsive as anyone else's, though a good deal less aggressive than Ahab's. In the midst of the most apparently dispassionate of all appreciations of natural beauty and the self-subsistence of other living things, that of the "young Leviathan amours in the deep," he is yet able to exercise the process of self-imaging in the subaqueous paradise beneath him:

> But even so, amid the tornadoed Atlantic of my being, do I myself still for ever centrally disport in mute calm; and while ponderous planets of unwaning woe revolve around me, deep down and deep inland there I still bathe me in eternal mildness of joy.
>
> (Ch. 87, p. 498)

Joy again, and as so often in this book, it is of the implicitly sexual sort. Ishmael is, however, a more open spirit than I might seem to be suggesting here. He sees the agony of the dying whale, even as he sees also "enough to appal the stoutest man who so pitied" (ch. 81, p. 462), and above all perhaps he asserts the criminality of the aspiration towards completion and full utterance, its blasphemous impossibility: "I promise nothing complete; because any human thing supposed to be complete, must for that very reason infallibly be faulty" (ch. 32, p. 229).

The locus of this quest for completion in the logic of phallicism, seen already in Ahab, is intuited more academically by Ishmael too, his

> cetological System standing thus unfinished, even as the great Cathedral of Cologne was left, with the crane still standing upon the top of the uncompleted tower. For small erections may be finished by their first architects; grand ones, true ones, ever leave the copestone to posterity. God keep me from ever completing anything. This whole book is but a draught—nay, but the draught of a draught. Oh, Time, Strength, Cash, and Patience!
>
> (Ch. 32, p. 241)

Melville seems to have chosen the richer of the two spellings open to him. The word *draught* occupies seven columns in the *OED*, and most of its meanings can be played into this passage and the book from which it comes. The process of definition is itself a vortex drawing us away from the aspiration to "finish" which the passage as a whole comments upon. The writer's art, positioned between first drafts and bank drafts (to use the more usual modern spelling), is itself defined within the metaphysical predicament of unfinishing, relief from which may be found in the draught of poison or the draught of wine. And is it all an exhalation of air, consigned to a privy? Thus all master builders?

The unfinishing goes on, and the mandatory incompletion of great erections touches on the traditional connection of sexual self-consciousness with the myth of the fall of man. Incompletion and endless aspiration are the fate of man outside Eden (women less so!), just as the sexual identity is thrust upon his conscience by the knowledge of transgression. At the level of the whaling industry as a whole (itself an image of territorial expansion and man's attempt to discipline nature, to cultivate or exploit the unparadisal earth), incompletion is reflected again in Ishmael's faith that the whale will *survive*. Ironic as it may seem to us today, he contrasts the whale with the buffalo, already as good as extinct with the progress of America's push westwards, and concludes that it will fare otherwise, and that it possesses the means to "bid defiance to all pursuit from man" (ch. 105, p. 573). Not only will it elude definition, Ishmael seems to suggest, but also man's pursuit to destroy it and to convert it completely to his purposes. This enables the whale, and Moby-Dick in particular, to function in the book as a rebuttal of both man's commercial greed and his possessive imagination. There will be something left when the whalers of this world have finished—something analogous, perhaps, to those "charms" and "mysteries" of which Melville spoke in the passage that stands as the epigraph to this chapter. Moby-Dick always has a life of his own. At one time he seems malevolent and purposeful, in ways that the human imagination can identify, at another he behaves in a way that speaks for utter indifference and self-containment, outside the scope of mankind's intentional projections. He is the fetish who is, like all fetishes, both admired and hated (or feared), but he also earns from Ishmael an independence from such a dialectic. Insofar as he is *not* destroyed, then the human quest itself comes to be, perversely, tinged with the heroism of a challenge to the unknowable and the impossible. Ishmael, in consequence, need never be quite the completely innocent observer touched on by Nietzsche at the opening of *The Will to Power*:

> He that speaks here, conversely, has done nothing so far but reflect: a philosopher and solitary by instinct, who has found his advantage in standing aside and outside, in patience, in procrastination, in staying behind . . . the first perfect nihilist of Europe who, however, has even now lived through the whole of nihilism, to the end, leaving it behind, outside himself.[7]

He is indeed rewarded for his comparative effacement from the scene of critical action and critical transgression by being allowed to fall behind, to survive both whales and sharks, and to tell his tale. He is the orphan picked up by the *Rachel* at the end of the book. And, if his name alludes to the wild outcast of Genesis, 16:12, invoked already in Fenimore Cooper's *The Prairie*, must this not be an ironic identification as applied to this whimsical sailor, who survives buoyed up on a floating coffin to tell his tale?

But despite these intimations of the incorporeal, Ishmael is not Nietzsche's "perfect nihilist." He too is a hunter of whales, and he is in admiration of Ahab's hatred of and search for that "inscrutable thing" (ch. 36, p. 262) he sees in the white whale. For Ahab offers the demonic (and potentially creative) prospect of it *not* being necessary to accept our shortcomings. The obverse of the energy of destruction is always that of civilization:

> But, as in his narrow-flowing monomania, not one jot of Ahab's broad madness had been left behind; so in that broad madness, not one jot of his great natural intellect had perished. That before living agent, now became the living instrument.

(Ch. 41, p. 284)

Agent to instrument, obscure, generative radical to utilitarian tool, idea to image, spirit to matter. Ahab's acts speak for the misapplication and reduction to fixity of what Coleridge called the "living Power and prime Agent of all human Perception" (*Biographia* 1. 202). Some degree of such fixity may, however, be necessary to all significant action. Ahab goes too far, so that he, "to that one end, did now possess a thousand fold more potency than ever he had sanely brought to bear upon any one reasonable object" (ch. 41, p. 284).

It is at least open to question, however, whether Ishmael goes far enough; for at times it seems close to the heart of Melville's ethic that we cannot live without significant action and the risks of transgression it involves. This deploying of active consciousness always exists in a state of tension for the Romantic and post-Romantic mind, and the argument for its necessity, as we have seen, must always draw a line to prevent itself approving of the more dangerous aspects of the Protestant aspiration, ever trying to complete itself into a prelapsarian state, to regain what it has (theorized as) inexorably lost. Just as a measure of this desire seems to be essential to all alternative constructions of order—and all orderings are constructed—so an excess of it directed at any one principle or component of such order alienates its possessor both from himself and from his community. The theory of knowledge in which this situation is contained insists on the presence of delirium at both ends of its spectrum. At one, there looms the prospect of monomania and fixation; at the other, random sensibility whose items are unconnected by *any* principle of succession or coherence. The Romantic ethic, as it appears in Wordsworth's idea of the imagination, and in Schiller's of the aesthetic, insists in return on the mobile occupation of the middle ground between.

If there is a place for asking the question about whether Ishmael goes far enough—and I would not myself weight the novel in this direction—then it is created, as I have said, in part and perhaps largely because Moby-Dick *survives* to be sought again; he is not destroyed by the various species of human figurings, whether commercial or metaphysical. Ahab does convert his own "living agent" into a mere instrument, but he is not ultimately able to incorporate Moby-Dick into that conspiracy of self-consolidation. If he were, then we would have a precise example of the reifying function of the labor process as it is specified by Marx:

> In the labour process, therefore, man's activity, *via* the instruments of labour, effects an alteration in the object of labour which was intended from the outset. The process is extinguished in the product. The product of the process is a use-value, a piece of natural material adapted to human needs by means of a change in its form. Labour has become bound up in its object: labour has been objectified, the object has been worked on. What on the side of the worker appeared in the form of unrest [*Unruhe*] now appears, on the side of the product,

in the form of being [*Sein*], as a fixed, immobile characteristic. The worker has spun, and the product is a spinning.

(*Capital*, p. 287)

Ahab, in these terms, is the unsuccessful "worker" who is not able to transform the natural material into the desired product. Moby-Dick does not undergo any alteration; if he has a "being," then it is a fluent, indeterminate one, ever challenging and open to challenge. Ahab's energies in fact rebound upon himself, and the way in which *his* labor becomes "bound up" is, as we have seen, somewhat literal; he is strangled by a line from the whale's body, in a commemoration of the alienated and detached nature of the "work" he has tried to do on his object. The whale's escape may be an image of the hope or faith or myth that man's energies as worker will not succeed in turning the world into a gallery of dead commodities.

The faith in this escape legitimizes, I think, the *horror vacui* that Ishmael seems to sense, at times, in the prospect of a life without Ahab and his kind. It renders less than catastrophic the "wild, mystical, sympathetical feeling" that allows him to affirm that "Ahab's quenchless feud seemed mine" (ch. 41, p. 276). In chapter 42, "The Whiteness of the Whale," Ishmael proceeds by conflating the accumulated cultural mythology of whiteness—"the intensifying agent in things the most appalling to mankind" (p. 295)—with the particular experience of the whale in a way that does not speak for any calling into question of his own self-consciousness; though of course we can provide that question for ourselves, insofar as he is a dramatic narrator. He is content to appeal to what he would have us take as instinct for the fearful intuition of "the nameless things of which the mystic sign gives forth such hints" (p. 295), and to a consensus of common experience for his final question: "Wonder ye then at the fiery hunt?" (p. 296).[8] We have already seen that the whiteness of the whale is in fact a figuring, a reading of the parts as the whole, and this suggests that it is a psychological compulsion we are witnessing in the interpretation of all things white:

> Or is it, that as in essence whiteness is not so much a color as the visible absence of color, and at the same time the concrete of all colors; is it for these reasons that there is such a dumb blankness, full of meaning, in a wide landscape of snows—a colorless, all-color of atheism from which we shrink?

(Pp. 295–96)

Atheism, not pantheism. In its tolerance of all superimposed inscriptions, all choices, as equally superficial, equally a *reflection* rather than a reading into or a glance within, the whiteness is a denial of the trick and turn of mind whereby the inquiring or idling spirit pretends that its impositions of differences and forms are authorized readings of the world outside. Hence atheism, the denial of a licence for seeing, and for sharing.

I cannot claim to be able to historicize firmly Ishmael's terror before the prospect (or figment) of pure whiteness, but there are interesting analogues in Wordsworth, and in Goethe's *Theory of Colours*. Goethe notes the disorganizing effects of whiteness; a bright object appears larger than a dark one of the same size, and while the dark one leaves the "organ in a state of repose," the bright one "excites it."[9] For

> the eye cannot for a moment remain in a particular state determined by the object it looks upon. On the contrary, it is forced to a sort of opposition, which, in contrasting extreme with extreme, intermediate degree with intermediate degree, at the same time combines these opposite impressions, and thus ever tends to a whole, whether the impressions are successive, or simultaneous and confined to one image.
>
> (P. 13)

Given that we construct form itself out of "light, shade, and colour" (p. xxxviii), we can see here the prospect of an epistemology based in the figured representations built out of the interchange between eye and object, much as we find it in Wordsworth. What is so violent about absolute whiteness is that, as an extreme state, it inspires an equally extreme reaction in the effort to compose a mediated wholeness; this is an instance of "the silent resistance which every vital principle is forced to exhibit when any definite or immutable state is presented to it" (p. 15). In this way, though to a lesser degree, every "decided colour does a certain violence to the eye, and forces the organ to opposition" (p. 25).

Similarly, whiteness for Wordsworth was a principle of disorganization. Absent in nature, in its pure form, except "in small objects," its introduction into the landscape by man "destroys the *gradations* of distance":

> Five or six white houses, scattered over a valley, by their obtrusiveness, dot the surface, and divide it into triangles, or other mathematical figures, haunting the eye, and disturbing that repose which might otherwise be perfect.
>
> (*Prose Works* 2. 216)

It subverts, in other words, that normative perspective that is based on the reading of depth and relation into the items placed before the eye, and placed in such a way as to contribute to the integration of that eye into the landscape beheld. Whiteness is in this sense a denial of power in its refusal to provide access to the depth of things, and to a principle of organization. Wordsworth's account of his journey through the Alps is pertinent here:

> That day we first
> Beheld the summit of Mont Blanc, and griev'd
> To have a soulless image on the eye
> Which had usurp'd upon a living thought
> That never more could be:
>
> (*The Prelude* 6. 452–56)

Here, the *mind*'s eye had prefigured the mountain into a symbolic presence, part in and for whole, an organizing figure of power. That was the "living thought," but experience, like Moby-Dick, fights back and insists on its difference; the actual optical sensation, being a poor substitute for what the mind has come to of itself, thus comes to be cast as a "soulless image." The 'real' is an *image* when set against the intending mind's fulsome anticipations. The imagination's aspiration to compose into unity is rebuked by contingency, as the landscape will not bear that kind of efficient selectiveness. Mont Blanc, in fact, proves itself unviable as a symbol, and also as a fetish, in that it will not allow the mind to elide its *difference* from matter; the act of giving meaning is thrown right back in the face of the donor. As we read on, it becomes clear that it is the reintroduction of the many for the one—the reversal of the process that the mind alone has tried to enact—which reconciles the poet's disappointment:

> the wondrous Vale
> Of Chamouny did, on the following dawn,
> With its dumb cataracts and streams of ice,
> A motionless array of mighty waves,
> Five rivers broad and vast, make rich amends,
> And reconcil'd us to realities.
>
> (6. 456–61)

The five make rich amends for the soleness and soullessness of the one. Wordsworth rebounds from blankness, from whiteness, to correct himself and, with the aid of an alternative nature, recreate the charitable space for human presence. Gradation is restored, albeit with the intimation of triteness in its prospect of embodied harmonies:

> There small birds warble from the leafy trees,
> The Eagle soareth in the element;
> There doth the reaper bind the yellow sheaf,
> The Maiden spread the haycock in the sun,
> While Winter like a tamed Lion walks
> Descending from the mountain to make sport
> Among the cottages by beds of flowers.
>
> (6. 462–68)

This somewhat humdrum listing of the items of the familiar landscape is a relief from the all-absorbing vacancy of whiteness, all-color and no color. Whiteness, like Hebrew theology, does not allow for representation. It is the image of infinity, and it is the death of the single self. If this is the coding of whiteness in *Moby-Dick*, then it makes the white whale both image and no-image. His shape and qualities attract the imagination, as his color thwarts and denies its operations; he is the fetish who compulsively attracts and inexorably disappoints, only to attract again. Whatever faltering there may be in Wordsworth's return to the lowlands, he does return. Ahab, and perhaps Ishmael too, remain with the soulless image, mesmerized, fixed, hateful, and worshipful. The "devious-cruising Rachel," searching for her own lost children, finds only another orphan in Ishmael (epilogue, p. 687). Loss replicates loss, and finding emphasizes that loss. But at least Moby-Dick survives.

CHAPTER 4

JOSEPH CONRAD: DIGGING FOR SILVER, DREAMING OF TRADE

Vicious demonstrations are the muniments and support of idols, and those which we possess in logic, merely subject and enslave the world to human thoughts, and thoughts to words.
Bacon, *Novum Organum*

It is safe to say that for the majority of mankind the superiority of geography over geometry lies in the appeal of its figures.
Conrad, *Last Essays*

To turn to Conrad is to encounter again that dialectic of activity and passivity, energy and energized self-incapacitation, which has throughout this inquiry surrounded the figurative activity in its various fluctuations between a deployed power over, and a subservience to, what is outside the individual mind. This subservience may be willed, or imposed from without, or both, with the latter working through the former. Metaphor, as the forging of new relations between things, and between people and things, is a potential tool of power for its originators, to the degree that it functions as a way of suppressing alternative figuring activity on the part of others. This it does by offering as real what can in fact be seen to be figured. The paradigm of fetishism, on the other hand, stresses the element of self-election in this process. Here, there is an active construction of a situation wherein the mind may abdicate its responsibility for an image it has itself created, and consequently close itself off from the possibility of renovation and change.

These two versions of enslavement by images of course are not incompatible; the repression of one person by another, or of one interest by another, may be effected either by removing all options of independent creativity, as Wordsworth saw city life to do, or by persuading others who have some element of choice to choose something that has already been chosen for them, though they may not know it. Ahab applies both pressures to his crew. He is their captain, and he actively enforces his habitual authority; but because he has broken the contract, he must also force the crew to "will" his goal for themselves, and to share his purpose from a position of self-determination. Similarly, with Ahab as with Dombey, the person in whose interest a structure of alienation is created and maintained will himself remain alienated, even as he receives the profits of those who work for him.

Mastery and slavery, then, in Melville as in Dickens, are at an equal remove from any essential or authentic self-satisfaction. Again, in both writers, the master-slave relation is organized around the commodity as a principle of exchange, but in such a way that the commodity has an imaginary as well as a material status. For those among Dickens's characters who remain potentially redeemable, as Dombey does, the cause of material self-interest is in tension with the requirements of the true inner identity, and thereby produces distorted and uncreative strategies of figuration; they are seen to be uncreative, and are eventually, at least in part, replaced by more generous images. In *Moby-Dick* mind and mammon are again in conflict, though in a different way. When Ishmael signs up for the crew of the *Pequod*, he does so under the guidance of Yojo, in a dismissal of the "sagacity" upon which he would otherwise prefer to depend (ch. 16, p. 163). Further, he is in no sense deceived by Peleg about the nature of whaling in general; it is explained to him as embodied in the fact that Ahab has "only one leg," and any romantic notions about seeing the world are deflated by his being shown the horizon, "exceedingly monotonous and forbidding" (pp. 167, 168). Ishmael is given some leading clues about what he is signing up for, and Peleg is no mere deceiving profiteer.

The *Pequod*, owned communally by a number of people among the "fighting Quakers" (p. 169) of Nantucket, but chiefly by Bildad and by Peleg, does indeed represent interests that seek to use Ahab as their tool. The "whalemen of America," we are told, produce annually "a well reaped harvest of $7,000,000" (ch. 24, p. 205), and the industry proceeds in a way not unmarked by the less admirable national characteristics:

> Herein it is the same with the American whale fishery as with the American army and military and merchant navies, and the engineering forces employed in the construction of the American Canals and Railroads. The same, I say, because in all these cases the native American liberally provides the brains, the rest of the world as generously supplying the muscles.
>
> (Ch. 27, p. 216)

Brains are provided by other brains, as Ahab by the owners; captains and crew alike may themselves be the tools of a society that decrees that whales must die in order to "illuminate the solemn churches that preach unconditional inoffensiveness by all to all" (ch. 81, p. 466). The whale must die, and someone must kill him. In such a way are all international relations but fast fish and loose fish (ch. 89, pp. 507–8), and so many religious and civic edifices but the commemorations of "standers of mast-heads" (ch. 35, p. 251).

There does not, however, seem to be much evidence for reading this book as any single-minded onslaught on the demands of the national economy. On the contrary, the commercial aspects of whaling are presented as inextricably interlocked with the imaginative drives of man. The Quakers, specifically, may start the quest, but the rest join in, finding therein (Starbuck excepted) a quest of their own. Moreover, Ahab turns the balance of the contract imposed by the commercial relation. No shipowner would seek to discourage some degree of imaginative investment in the trade, as a way of inciting added energies: "Nor is it so very unlikely, that far from distrusting his fitness for another whaling voyage, on account of such dark symptoms, the calculating people of that prudent isle were inclined to harbor the conceit, that for those very reasons he was all the better qualified and set on edge, for a pursuit so full of rage and wildness as the bloody hunt of whales" (ch. 41, p. 285). But Ahab goes overboard in more ways than one. In him, commerce is redigested by imagination, and imagination itself directed by harsh reality, to a degree that makes it all the more compulsively imaginary. The ship becomes the vehicle of Ahab's quest, as Ahab assumes the control that the owners purport to exercise over him. They—the ship, the crew, the owners—become *his* tools.

The complexity of trade and imagination in Conrad's writing is not generally heightened or centralized to the point that creates an Ahab. We are back in the old world again, a world singularly unfit for the production of potentially heroic figures. It is a less energetic world; or rather, the energies that do subsist, and that keep going the wheels of commerce and moral idealism, each fuelling the other, are more dissipated and therefore less prone to emergence in exemplary individuality. Conrad is, moreover, much less certain that Moby-Dick is a survivor. Melville, or Ishmael, had described the Sunda straits, separating Sumatra from Java, as the gateway to "some vast walled empire" whose contents seemed by the very "formation of the land" to have the appearance, "however ineffectual, of being guarded from the all-grasping western world" (ch. 87, p. 488). Conrad's novels of the colonial experience may be taken as a testament to the ineffectuality of that appearance.

They are the extension into empire of the old world that Dickens had left us with at the end of *Hard Times*. There, however, Sissy Jupe is constituted as the center of a sympathetic micro-community based on familial interaction and benevolent femininity. She will spread sweetness and light outward from a basis in a clearly perceived intuition of what is most positive and most threatening in life. She will try "to know her humbler fellow creatures, and to beautify their lives of machinery and reality with those imaginative graces and delights, without which the heart of infancy will wither up, the sturdiest physical manhood will be morally stark death, and the plainest national prosperity figures can show, will be the Writing on the Wall . . . " (3. ch. 9, p. 165). We are almost back in a pre-Romantic formulation of the function of imagination and the figurative as embellishment or ornamentation upon a preestablished and unreconstructed reality; metaphor relieves us from the plainness of the truth, and enlivens its reference to fact. I take it that we are to register no false consciousness on Sissy's part; she sees that the mechanical has been firmly encoded as the real, and sets out to provide a creative if limited alternative to it. This may be the best possible alternative, without going through the complete social revolution that Dickens, at the last, always fails to advocate. It may not be much, but it is something.

With Conrad, the odds on the genesis or survival of even such minimal centers of concentrated humanity as Sissy Jupe's family seem very much shorter. In Conrad's novels there are few women, and almost no children. The enlightened family grouping, fragile enough in Dickens because of his intuition about the repressive operations of families—Dorrits, Brays, Jellybys, Turveydrops, and so forth—is no longer represented, and least of all is it to be found in the novels of colonialism, if I may so term them, which I shall discuss here.

The constant presence throughout these novels and tales is that of commerce. Adam Smith had related the incidence of the division of labor to a "propensity in human nature" to "truck, barter, and exchange one thing for another" (*Wealth of Nations*, p. 25). In Conrad, it is strongly suggested that any implications of innatism in this statement of Smith's are to be qualified by its truth to masculine rather than feminine nature. There is a good deal of evidence to suggest that, in the subtlest way, Conrad intuits a relation between the figurative and commercial imaginations and the compulsion to self-completion in the male psyche. The phallicism so boldly put forward by Melville is considerably occluded, but remains implicitly central to a wider narcissism historically played out over the face of the uncharted world.

The intensity of the relation Conrad remarks between commerce and imagination is relentless, and probably obvious to the reader. The first page of the first novel, *Almayer's Folly* (1895), offers a correspondence between world-as-seen and obsessional idea in Almayer's enjoyment of the sunset. As he sees the "glowing gold tinge on the waters," so his thoughts are "often busy with gold."[1] The doubling effect is much less intense and enclosing than it is between Ahab and Moby-Dick, each reflecting the prominent attributes of the other in a world of neurotic reduplication (whether for Ishmael or for Ahab), but the aspiration remains at root the same. Blake had earlier specified a contrast between imaginative and intentional vision in terms that ironize the same mercantile cast of mind attributed to Almayer:

> What it will be Questiond When the Sun rises do you not see a round Disk of fire somewhat like a Guinea O no no I see an Innumerable company of the Heavenly host crying Holy Holy Holy is the Lord God Almighty.
>
> (*Poetry & Prose*, p. 555)

A man with money on his mind sees money. Almayer's fantasies are based on what he thinks he lacks, and this he shares with his neighbors: "The coast population of Borneo believes implicitly in diamonds of fabulous value, in gold mines of enormous richness in the interior. And all those imaginings are heightened by the difficulty of penetrating far inland" (ch.

3, p. 39). Absence is the source of imagination, and imagination the rationale for and corrollary of exploitation and invasion. Nostromo speaks of
treasure as something that

> fastens upon a man's mind. He will pray and blaspheme and still persevere, and
> will curse the day he ever heard of it, and will let his last hour come upon him
> unawares, still believing that he missed it only by a foot. He will see it every time
> he closes his eyes.
>
> (*N* 3. ch. 9, p. 460)

Treasure is the goal that maintains the structure of desire. In fact, for Nostromo, the goal is achieved, but it turns out to be something different from
what it promises. Its conversion from the imagined into the real is not
successful. Because no one else must know that he possesses it, the treasure
cannot be exchanged, and therefore cannot exist as a genuine commodity:

> Nostromo had been growing rich very slowly . . . to become the slave of a
> treasure with full self-knowledge is an occurrence rare and mentally disturbing.
> But it was also in a great part because of the difficulty of converting it into a form
> in which it could become available.
>
> (3. ch. 12, p. 523)

The silver, then, must remain a dissappointing fetish, an isolated and useless object of a strictly private relationship. Far from providing the completion that might at some subliminal level have been the function of its
creation as an obsession in Nostromo's mind, it actually robs him of experience by encouraging or necessitating the subordination of other aspects
of life. Thus he is forced to repress and consciously direct his sexuality, and
to exploit his relation to Viola's daughters in order to "grow rich quicker"
(3. ch. 12, p. 529). The image, the 'means by which,' has become the end,
the thing in itself and 'for which.' It imposes an impossible consistency
upon his behavior, and its very presence bespeaks the alienation of the
inner man: "His courage, his magnificence, his leisure, his work, everything was as before, only everything was a sham. But the treasure was real"
(3. ch. 12, pp. 523–24). He courts Linda instead of Giselle, who is the
focus of his natural inclinations, because he is "afraid of being forbidden
the island," and yet it is only Giselle who can convert "his weary subjec-
tion to that dead thing into an exulting conviction of his power" (3. ch. 12,
pp. 531, 541). Even here, we notice, Nostromo's resort is to a self-gratifying
emotion, that of power; it would seem that the very compulsion that
makes him fasten on the treasure as a fetish must ruin also any potential
for the acceptance of the incompletion that would constitute an authentic
and creative heterosexual bond.

Nostromo's fate demonstrates that even possession of what has been
figuratively misendowed with essential reality does not mitigate that desire responsible for the genesis of the fetishistic process itself. This suggests
that the goal is itself illusory, strictly *as* a goal. That this quest is some-

thing deeper and more compulsive than mere greed, or at least has become so (for Conrad offers no sure statement of first causes), is intimated in the frequent conflations of the images of profit and of imagination. Tom Lingard is "always in search of new markets for his cargoes—not so much for profit as for the pleasure of finding them" (*OI* 1. ch. 2, p. 14). The southern seas in *Lord Jim* are plied by the *Pelion* and the *Ossa*, named after the tools employed by the giants in their attempts to scale heaven and make war on the gods, and the providers of the timber for Jason's ships— Jason, that classical prototype of mercantile man, that confounder of mammon and imagination. In *Heart of Darkness* the "white patch" on the maps of Marlow's youth has "become a place of darkness," and the darkness has accrued by its being caught up by "the merry dance of death and trade" masquerading as white civilization (ch. 1, pp. 52, 62). Kurtz's visions of the trading posts as centers for "humanizing, improving, instructing" (ch. 2, p. 91), are to be set against Marlow's perception that "the Company was run for profit" (ch. 1, p. 59). Charles Gould subsists by the successful interdetermination of the imagined and the real, as "the Idealist-creator of Material Interests" (*N*, p. xi). According to Decoud, he is the possessor of "the greatest fact in the whole of South America, perhaps," and it has become for him "a part of some fairy tale," a clothing of "personal desires with a shining robe of silk and jewels" (2. ch. 6, pp. 214, 215, 218). A right royal investiture, indeed, and one embraced also by Gould's American backer, Holroyd, who is bitten by the same bug:

> In the San Tomé mine he had found the imaginative satisfaction which other minds would get from drama, from art, or from a risky and fascinating sport. It was a special form of the great man's extravagance, sanctioned by a moral intention, big enough to flatter his vanity.
>
> (3. ch. 4, p. 374)

This is often presented as a compulsion specific or at least common to the whites races, this filling out of greed by the operations of the creative or moral imagination. Decoud describes the Englishman as one who "cannot act or exist without idealizing every simple feeling, desire, or achievement" (2. ch. 6, pp. 214–15). Patusan, a place "known by name to some few, very few, in the mercantile world" (*LJ*, ch. 21, p. 218), and comparatively unexploited by whites, operates according to a much less exalted estimation of trade, one "indistinguishable from the commonest forms of robbery" (ch. 25, p. 257), as opposed to the more sophisticated but no less destructive species of power imported by Jim himself.

In general, the structure of commerce is maintained by a structure of racism, and by a corollary displacement or humiliation of the woman. Almayer's terror at the prospect of his daughter's marriage to a native (*AF*, ch. 11, p. 184), and Willems's loss of control and self-esteem before Aïssa, indicate both the destructiveness and the fragility of white suprematism:

> He seemed to be surrendering to a wild creature the unstained purity of his life, of his race, and of his civilization. He had a notion of being lost among shapeless things that were dangerous and ghastly.
>
> (*OI* 1. ch. 7, p. 80)

Shapeless things, unfixed things, are threatening. Dombey saw this threat, or failed to see it, in the potential wanderings of the "little image." Here it is the province of the other race, and of the woman. Racism is both crude and sophisticated. The racism of the crew of the *Patna*, or of Captain Robinson in his readiness to drive coolies to the death to exploit guano on lonely islands (*LJ*, ch. 14, p. 166), or of Schomberg and Ricardo in their view of life as a "play of shadows the dominant race could walk through unaffected and disregarded in the pursuit of its incomprehensible aims and needs" (*V* 2. ch. 8, p. 167), is of the cruder sort. But there is more than a hint of a more sophisticated and romantic racial idealism in Marlow's memory of Jim as a "tiny white speck, that seemed to catch all the light left in a darkened world" (*LJ*, ch. 35, p. 336), especially when it is set in the context of his mystified view of the relation of commerce and moral imagination. The Dutch and English traders prepared to "cut each other's throats" for a bag of pepper are seen as "heroic" but also "pathetic" (ch. 22, p. 226); and yet to us

> their less tried successors, they appear magnified, not as agents of trade but as instruments of a recorded destiny, pushing out into the unknown in obedience to an inward voice, to an impulse beating in the blood, to a dream of the future. They were wonderful; and it must be owned they were ready for the wonderful. They recorded it complacently in their sufferings, in the aspect of the seas, in the customs of strange nations, in the glory of splendid rulers.
>
> (P. 227)

Was that "inward voice" an ideal "dream of the future," or an amoral Schopenhauerian "impulse beating in the blood"? Perhaps it was both; but which came first? Marlow, through the haze of time and the prism of romance, is anxious to validate their efforts as deriving from more than "mere greed." But the authority of his reconstruction of history is certainly challenged by his tendency to reconstruct Jim—a piece of the present, though mediated to us through memory—as a function of his own fears and aspirations, a companionable form. At the beginning of *Heart of Darkness* Marlow's notions follow a similar pattern: "The conquest of the earth, which mostly means the taking it away from those who have a different complexion or slightly flatter noses than ourselves, is not a pretty thing when you look into it too much. What redeems it is the idea only" (ch. 1. pp. 50–51). However, as Marlow himself comes to recognize, these reflections are quite out of step with what he actually finds in Africa. Kurtz's report makes him "tingle with enthusiasm" only until he comes upon the final, unofficial postscript: "Exterminate all the brutes!" (ch. 2, p. 118).

It is hard to be sure (perhaps we are not meant to be sure) how much if any of Marlow's conflation of trade and imagination, avarice and idealism, is to be ascribed to Conrad in his own voice. The short essay "Geography and Some Explorers" does, however, provide at least a clue. Here, Conrad makes a clear distinction between those voyagers who were prompted by "the idea of lucre in some form, the desire of trade or the desire of loot, disguised in more or less fine words," and those "whose only object was the search for truth."[2] Cook and Franklin belonged to this latter class, practicing what Conrad calls "militant geography" (see, for example, pp. 28, 31), a selfless pursuit of facts for their own sakes. Given the force of this distinction in Conrad's own voice, it may be a clue worth pondering that Marlow gets the two categories mixed up, seeming to apportion to the looters the moral affirmation strictly belonging to the militants.

I shall return to Marlow's case later in this account. He seems to remain undecided about the source and nature of this conjunction in Kurtz. At one point he is quite clear about the nature of the Company's ambitions, at another he seems to believe that he is on the track of his "idea" and that Kurtz's deviations might have been forced upon him by the pressures of an atavistic environment. Before exploring this further, it is worth noticing that there are elsewhere strong suggestions that the configured structure of imaginative commerce may be nothing more than a mystification of white masculine energies and desires. It is the women who deliver the strongest denunciations of the demands of trade and profit. Nina Almayer, who belongs to both races, is quite clear in her evaluation. She sees in both races

> the same manifestations of love and hate and of sordid greed chasing the uncertain dollar in all its multifarious and vanishing shapes. To her resolute nature, however, after all these years, the savage and uncompromising sincerity of purpose shown by her Malay kinsmen seemed at least preferable to the sleek hypocrisy, to the polite disguises, to the virtuous pretences of such white people as she had had the misfortune to come in contact with.
>
> (*AF*, ch. 3, p. 43)

Aïssa cannot understand Willems's impulse to degrade her, and she stands amazed before "that man born in the land of violence and of evil wherefrom nothing but misfortune comes to those who are not white" (*OI* 2. ch. 6, p. 153). Insofar as the female perception thus threatens the models of the world created by and for the males, then the women must be ignored or excluded. Marlow subscribes to this exclusion, I think, in a way that the logic of the tales he tells us does not. In commenting that "They—the women I mean—are out of it—should be out of it. We must help them to stay in that beautiful world of their own, lest ours gets worse" (*HD*, ch. 2, p. 115), he can be seen to be subscribing to the status quo (and to the consequent fetishization of the woman), the very insistence on difference that allows the male world to remain as it is. He thus contributes to the survival of a situation that he appears to lament, and surreptitiously inhibits the possibilities for reconstruction.

For Marlow as a 'character,' the conviction of difference appears at times to be based on a sense of the immovability of the world founded in the reciprocally reinforcing play of trade and imagination, as he opines:

> Our common fate fastens upon the women with a peculiar cruelty. It does not punish like a master, but inflicts lingering torment, as if to gratify a secret, unappeasable spite. One would think that, appointed to rule on earth, it seeks to revenge itself upon the beings that come nearest to rising above the trammels of earthly caution; for it is only women who manage to put at times into their love an element just palpable enough to give one a fright—an extra-terrestrial touch.
>
> (*LJ*, ch. 28, p. 277)

Perhaps Marlow gives himself away; it gives him a "fright." The passage might have been written for Mrs. Gould, who achieves by her "feminine" intelligence a kind of "conquest" of Sulaco, "simply by lighting the way for her unselfishness and sympathy." Her nature lacks "even the most legitimate touch of materialism" (*N* 1. ch. 6, pp. 67, 75). The Coleridgean ideal now reposes in the woman, but her presence counts for almost nothing in the world of Costaguana, except in the mute hearts of a few admirers. Her perception is exactly antithetical to that of her husband and the ruling interest, imprisoned as it is within the wider world of male self-regard. As such, it cannot surface:

> The fate of the San Tomé mine was lying heavy upon her heart. It was a long time now since she had begun to fear it. It had been an idea. She had watched it with misgivings turning into a fetish, and now the fetish had grown into a monstrous and crushing weight. It was as if the inspiration of their early years had left her heart to turn into a wall of silver-bricks, erected by the silent work of evil spirits, between her and her husband. He seemed to dwell alone within a circumvallation of precious metal, leaving her outside with her school, her hospital, the sick mothers, and the feeble old men, mere insignificant vestiges of the initial inspiration. "Those poor people!" she murmured to herself.
>
> (2. ch. 6, pp. 221–22)[3]

As idea turns to fetish and fetish to material and imaginative monopoly, Mrs. Gould is squeezed out along with the remaindered servants of capital. She sees but cannot cure the sexual alienation, enacted by the fetish, between her and her husband, which reproduces itself upon those other elements of the population who are 'feminized' into impotence. She sees the mountain

> hanging over the Campo, over the whole land, feared, hated, wealthy; more soulless than any tyrant, more pitiless and autocratic than the worst Govern-

ment; ready to crush innumerable lives in the expansion of its greatness. He did not see it. He could not see it.

(3. ch. 11, p. 521)

Much more soulless, also, than Wordsworth's "soulless image," for this mountain has been more fully and successfully endowed with reified identity, more fully imagined as the real. It is the source of the silver, and it is thus the material whole to which Charles Gould relates as efficient part, as metonymically attached worshipper. Mrs. Gould occupies a differently figured world, but because it has no support and stands in conflict with that of the possessors of power, it is not an equal world. It remains a subdued counterpoint that will be destroyed whenever it threatens to emerge into melody.

Willems and Aïssa also stand "each the centre of dissimilar and distant horizons; standing each on a different earth, under a different sky." Whilst she recalls his romantic appearance and physical presence as the "beginning of her power," he remembers

> the quaysides and the warehouses; the excitement of a life in a whirl of silver coins; the glorious uncertainty of a money hunt; his numerous successes, the lost possibilities of wealth and consequent glory. She, a woman, was the victim of her heart, of her woman's belief that there is nothing in the world but love—the everlasting thing. He was the victim of his strange principles, of his continence, of his blind belief in himself, of his solemn veneration for the voice of his boundless ignorance.

(OI 5. ch. 3, pp. 333–34)

Her reality is at least a resident of the heart and the spirit, and not a property of the outward image or fetish. In this, as in so many of Conrad's novels of empire, woman exists for man primarily as part of the network of alienated exchange which constitutes the commercial imagination. Almayer marries his wife at the dictate of a vision of "great piles of shining guilders" (*AF*, ch. 1, p. 10).

Karain, in the story to which he gives his name, also exemplifies the genesis of the commitment to substitution. He is always described as functioning within a dense context of objects, metonymic images of power, "dressed splendidly for his part" (*TU*, ch. 1, p. 6), and "incomparably faithful to the illusions of the stage" (p. 9). Even his follower comes to seem "something inanimate, as part of our friend's trappings of state—like that sword he had carried, or the fringed red umbrella displayed during an official progress" (ch. 3, pp. 19–20). As the story unfolds, we learn that this obsession with attributes and emblems follows on from an earlier loss of authentic human relations; the loss of a woman and the murder of a friend. Karain is not white, of course, and perhaps this is why his life suggests the *evolution* of the substitution of things for persons; Almayer cannot show this as a process, because he seems to have been born to it as a way of life.

A more subtle form of misrepresentation appears in Jim's relation to his native bride; subtle in that it qualifies the positive estimation that he obviously intends. He christens her "Jewel"—the men often do the naming—as she is indeed an ornament or attribute of his ideal self-image. Appropriately, her father "regarded himself as entitled to some money in exchange for the girl" (*LJ*, ch. 34, p. 327); she is caught in a network of exchange which recognizes her as a commodity, whether it be in cash or in imagination. Because of her name, given to her by Jim, as the product of a contemplation that is certainly implicitly fetishistic, even as it is sincere, she becomes the focus of a rumor specifying the existence of a real treasure. Marlow discovers that "a story was travelling slowly down the coast about a mysterious white man in Patusan who had got hold of an extraordinary gem—namely, an emerald of an enormous size, and altogether priceless" (ch. 28, p. 280). This jewel, it is further rumored, is worn concealed upon the bosom of the tall girl who is his constant companion. This rumor is merely a cruder or more overt example of the ideal-materialization that Jim himself has already enacted, and there is a deeper complicity within the apparent difference in the two attitudes to her. By way of the name that is the sign of her status as an attribute of Jim's egotism, she has become for the locals the vehicle of a real wealth that they imagine. It is a proper recognition of her status; she is the vehicle of imaginary value from both sides.

In the case of Lord Jim in particular, there is a tempting historical and thematic analogy to be drawn between Conrad's writing and Freud's ideas on fetishism and narcissism. To begin with, in Freud, both these syndromes are firmly incorporated as within the normal; they are not exiled to a space of exclusion, and thus negated, but are argued to be present to some degree in all of us: "an unbroken chain bridges the gap between the neuroses in all their manifestations and normality."[4] Similarly, in the specific case of narcissism, there is a "primary narcissism in everyone," and the "human being remains to some extent narcissistic even after he has found external objects for his libido" (14. 88; 13. 89). This inclusion, which of course affects the relation of patient and analyst, parallels, in a sense, the elision of distinctions Conrad performs between Marlow and Jim, narrator and object of narration. Marlow 'is' Jim in that he sees himself reflected from him, and Jim 'is' Marlow insofar as his identity takes form for the reader (as I shall try to show in what follows) as a function of Marlow's intentional consciousness. Jim's pathology, if such it be, takes on meaning because of what it touches off in Marlow.

More specifically, Jim reflects what Freud implicitly suggests about the consanguinity of fetishism and narcissism. As early as 1905 Freud defined *fetishism* as the substitution of a *part* of the body, or "some inanimate object which bears an assignable relation to the person whom it replaces and preferably to that person's sexuality," for the sexual object (7. 153). The later arguments about fetishism relate it particularly to phallicism (as the earlier anthropological theorists had), in that the fetish is consequent upon the 'loss' of the mother's penis; that is, upon the intuition that she does not have one. This absence in the mother poses the threat that the male child may also lose his penis, and the choice of the fetish compensates for this, by fixing upon an external object that both offers permanence in the imaginary and deflects attention from the real. As such, it is always based on a self-reflecting motive, that of "narcissism" (21. 153). Freud offers a famous aside on this subject which relates directly to earlier parts of this book: "In later life a grown man may perhaps experience a similar panic when the cry goes up that Throne and Altar are in danger, and similar illogical consequences will ensue" (21. 53). The immediate point here, however, is that fetishism always supposes an aversion to the real female genitals (and by extension, to the female), because of the threat of loss that they represent. I do not want to argue for the truth or falsehood of Freud's position, but it does comment interestingly on the operations of Jim's and/or Marlow's mind as we infer them from Conrad's novel. The choice of the name "Jewel" is a gesture of proffered substitution, in language, a fixing upon an inanimate object as the focus of desire and attention; an object, moreover, which is recognized as a commodity by the rest of the world. The fixity of the name replaces the threat or unpredictability of experience. Jewel thus becomes a thing to be displayed, and a thing that could not feel; the referent is usurped by the sign. She is another version of the perfection Stein finds in his butterflies, capturable only in death.[5]

Further clues about the nature of Jim's condition can be adduced from Freud's 1914 paper "On Narcissism" (14. 69–102). Here, the original interruption of the primary narcissism that is in us all (at least, the *men*!) is identified with the onset of the castration complex (p. 92). We may infer from this, though Freud does not spell it out, that subsequent narcissistic activity will tend to function through the fetish, which also has its roots in the threatened loss of the genital organ. What Freud goes on to say about narcissism is particularly pertinent to Jim. Adult narcissism is fuelled by an "ideal ego" that becomes "the target of the self-love which was enjoyed in childhood by the actual ego" (p. 94). The presence of this ideal "heightens the demands of the ego and is the most powerful factor favouring repression." It does not automatically produce sublimation, which is absent in neurotics; such persons demonstrate the incidence of a "special psychical agency" that "watches" the "actual ego" and measures it by the demands of the ideal. They therefore exhibit great anxieties about "being *watched*" (p. 95). Public opinion can thus seem an extension of parental control and supervision; Jim is as anxious to hide his shame from coming to his father's door as he is to hide from the public eye in general, the one perhaps being a means to the other. The way in which Jim will disappear at the mere mention of his case is testimony to this hypersensitivity. The woman is an image, specified in the name, so that he will indeed leave "a living woman to celebrate his pitiless wedding with a shadowy ideal of conduct" (ch. 45, p. 416).

We can turn to another novel for evidence of what happens, even in a case considerably less tortured than Jim's, when the woman rises above the rôle to which she is assigned in the male imagination, and begins to take on the position of an equal, becoming the possessor of a world of rival figures. In *The Rescue*, Edith Travers intrudes into a world where Lingard, the exemplary white male, has established for himself a delicate and mostly benevolent suprematism and an interracial trust based on loyalty to function. The efficient female in Lingard's life has hitherto always been his ship:

> He was aware that his little vessel could give him something not to be had from anybody or anything in the world; something specially his own. The dependence of that solid man of bone and muscle on that obedient thing of wood and iron, acquired from that feeling the mysterious dignity of love. She—the craft—had all the qualities of a living thing: speed, obedience, trustworthiness, endurance, beauty, capacity to do and to suffer—all but life. He—the man—was the inspirer of that thing that to him seemed the most perfect of its kind.
>
> (1. ch. 1, p. 11)

Lingard later reveals this marriage of man and matter as the source of his power:

> They fear the brig because when I am on board her, the brig and I are one. An armed man—don't you see? Without the brig I am disarmed, without me she can't strike.
>
> (4. ch. 4, pp. 226–27)

The relation of man to machine is here described in terms of a transferred sexuality, man to woman, purified of the dialectic of interaction which must make it at least partly inefficient and incomplete when it remains a *real* relation between man and woman. Mrs. Travers arrives as the real female and is thus a challenge to the figure on which Lingard subsists, and which is essential to his reputation. She herself has married a much reduced version of socialized masculinity, a man who is satisfied with "her beauty, her brilliance, and her useful connections," but who does not possess "a single true emotion" (3. ch. 6, p. 152). Edith Travers has a much larger rôle than have either Jewel or Mrs. Gould, but this active contribution seems only to emphasize Conrad's pessimism about the prospects for a positive or redeeming relation between the sexes. She is a threat to the society Lingard has built up around himself; she causes him to forget, in his infatuation, his truest friends—"For the second time he discovered that he had forgotten the existence of Hassim and Immada" (4. ch. 5, p. 259)—and her holding on to the ring at the important moment is not a simple crime but, for Lingard, a symbol of his already being lost to the old world of truth and trustworthiness. He cannot cope with the demands made upon his emotions and imagination by the presence of the real female, as the sensitive interracial harmony cannot cope with the intrusion of more white people and their insidious demands on Lingard's racial loyalties. That the 'affair' between the two of them is not even consummated, because of class differences, fierce habits, and natural shyness, is a further irony and another negative force keeping man from woman.

Willems too had found that the real female could not be held within the efficient categories of profit and public reputation, his real goals. Aïssa, it will be remembered, threatens the "unstained purity" of his image of himself—the vocabulary of virginity is not accidental—by her intimation of the polymorphous and the uncontrollable, "shapeless things that were dangerous and ghastly" (*OI* 1. ch. 7, p. 80). Almayer, having made his mercantile marriage, finds his wife reverting to what seems to him an "original savagery" at the same time that trade in Sambir proves to be something less manageable than he had hoped for: "He could not guide Patalolo, control the irrepressible old Sahamin, or restrain the youthful vagaries of the fierce Bahassoen with pen, ink and paper. He found no successful magic in the blank pages of his ledgers; and gradually he lost his old point of view in the saner appreciation of his situation. The room known as the office became neglected then like a temple of an exploded superstition" (*OI* 5. ch. 1, p. 300). The little images, the woman and the traders, revolt and wander out of the power of the temple of commerce and its priest, the white male narcissist. The language of religious or magical identity occurs often in the descriptions of imaginary power sought or assumed by Almayer and his kind. Willems, in his relation to the Da Souzas, "loved to breathe the coarse incense they offered before the shrine of the successful white man," and Lingard becomes "Rajah Laut—the King of the Sea" (*OI* 1. ch. 1, p. 4; ch. 2, p. 14). Jim has for the inhabitants of Patusan the "racial prestige and the reputation of invincible, supernatural power" (*LJ*, ch. 39, p. 361), and he is fetishized by Marlow too in his mood of romantic racism: "He dominated the forest, the secular gloom, the old mankind. He was like a figure set up on a pedestal, to represent in his persistent youth the power, and perhaps the virtues, of races that never grow old, that have emerged from the gloom" (ch. 26, p. 265). "I don't know why he should always have appeared to me symbolic," says Marlow.

The silver mine in *Nostromo* is also invested with magical and religious properties. The "idolatry" of the "dressed-up saints in the cathedral" is piously dismissed by Holroyd, but only in favor of a god who is a "sort of influential partner" (1. ch. 6, p. 71). Even the Indians worship the mine, a fact that Conrad explains with reference to exactly the imbalance between process and product which we have seen to be so central to the Romantic polemic against the more dangerous tendencies of the figurative: "They were proud of, and attached to, the mine. It had secured their confidence and belief. They invested it with a protecting and invincible virtue as though it were a fetish made by their own hands, for they were ignorant, and in other respects did not differ appreciably from the rest of mankind which puts infinite trust in its own creations" (3. ch. 6, p. 398). Silver, the "incorruptible metal" (2. ch. 8, p. 300), is the material corollary of Nostromo's reputation, from which he himself derives his identity, a situation intimated in his very name, "our man," the tool of ulterior interests, itself ironically the result of "Captain Mitchell's mispronunciation" (1. ch. 5, p. 43).

Heart of Darkness is so clearly an investigation of fetishism that it might seem redundant to point it out once again. Kurtz, the ivory worshipper, has a "lofty frontal bone" (another bodily displacement of the nature of Moby-Dick's hump?) and a head "impressively bald . . . like a ball—an ivory ball." He reflects, or projects, what he pursues, and in his pursuit of the external, in the exploitation of the forest—"You would think there was not a single tusk left"—he has himself "withered": "The wilderness . . . had taken him, loved him, embraced him, got into his veins, consumed his flesh, and sealed his soul to its own by the inconceivable ceremonies of some devilish initiation" (ch. 2, p. 115). Conrad is less explicit than Melville, but Kurtz is at least something of an Ahab in his desperate and obsessive search for ivory, and similarly, he exhibits a version of the wrinkled brow in his showing forth the Murdstone phrenology, the "lofty frontal bone," itself perhaps an image of or substitution for the lack that is intimated again in the "slim posts . . . roughly trimmed, and with their upper ends ornamented with round carved balls" (ch. 2, p. 121), both the actual products of Kurtz's pagan rituals and the figured forms of his own dismembering. (Dulaure, *Histoire* 1. 454ff., in his argument for the cult of the dead being the bridging point between fetishism and idolatry, had paid special attention to columns and tree trunks topped with human heads as phallic emblems.) Kurtz need not be thought of as literally impotent, of course, but the emblems of mutilation do image his state of mind.

And there is a further extension of the fetishistic in this story. Marlow, the narrator, at least as he is *seen*, "resembled an idol" (ch. 1, p. 46) to those listening to his tale, and his own propensity to mental idolatry is clearly detailed in his worship of ideas. In his view of the redeeming element of conquest, he asserts that

> What redeems it is the idea only. An idea at the back of it; not a sentimental pretence but an idea; and an unselfish belief in the idea—something you can set up, and bow down before, and offer a sacrifice to. . . .
>
> (Ch. 1, p. 51)

The setting up, the bowing down, and the sacrificing, enact the complete cycle of creation, self-suppression, and aggression which is the dance of death and trade, exploitation and desire. Marlow's is merely the most sophisticated of a series of mutually enclosing idolatries, and it encloses them all in the fabric of narration itself, as it tells of the Company which is a "whited sepulchre" and whose offices are "the biggest thing in the town" (ch. 1, p. 55); of the native woman who is all "barbarous ornaments," all attributes—"There was a low jingle, a glint of yellow metal, a sway of fringed draperies, and she stopped as if her heart had failed her" (ch. 3, pp. 135, 136); and, of course, of Kurtz himself. Marlow encloses a whole series of figures, and ends as he began, "in the pose of a meditating Buddha" (ch. 3, p. 162). People are constantly seeing each other as figures, facsimiles of ivory.

This is indeed a pattern in Conrad's writing. Willems and Aïssa look to Almayer "like figures carved with great precision of detail and highly finished by a skilful hand" (*OI* 4 ch. 5, p. 272). Mrs. Schomberg always appears "like an enthroned idol . . . like a figure made of wood," as befits her enforced subordination to her husband; she is "a very plain dummy, with an arrangement for bowing the head at times and smiling stupidly now and then" (*V* 1. ch. 5, pp. 39–40). Almayer's worship of his daughter enacts a process not dissimilar to Dombey's insistence on seeing himself in his child: he looks

> at that part of himself, at that small and unconscious particle of humanity that seemed to him to contain all his soul . . . he appeared strangely impressive and ecstatic: like a devout and mystic worshipper, adoring, transported and mute; burning incense before a shrine, a diaphanous shrine of a child-idol with closed eyes; before a pure and vapourous shrine of a small god—fragile, powerless, unconscious and sleeping.
>
> (*OI* 5. ch. 2, p. 320)

She seems to contain all his soul, and yet she is outside him, with a potential life of her own. Almayer and Willems live in the same exclusive world, in "the temple of self and the concentration of personal thought" (1. ch. 3, p. 31). Many of Conrad's male protagonists present a hard face to the world, and Stein's dead butterflies—"Something of me. The best" (*LJ*, ch. 20, p. 205)—are a humbler version of self-imaging than that evinced by others in the novel. Brierly projects "a surface as hard as granite" (ch. 6, p. 58) but reveals the inner insubstantiality of this by the suicide's death, having recognized his own companionship in Jim's predicament; at least, so we must assume. Jim himself, as we see him through Marlow, is forever in search of a "gorgeous virility" (ch. 3, p. 2), which he is to find only in death, in the "proud and unflinching glance" (ch. 45, p. 416) of his last act. Willems is more successfully or irredeemably given to the posture of firmness; "severe and unbending" before Aïssa's caresses, he becomes "as solid and motionless as one of the big trees of the surrounding forests" (*OI* 2. ch. 6, pp. 139, 140). In the same novel, Conrad becomes more explicit about the nature of the goal such behavior is ultimately aimed at:

> Consciously or unconsciously, men are proud of their firmness, steadfastness of purpose, directness of aim. They go straight towards their desire, to the accom-

plishment of virtue—sometimes of crime—in an uplifting persuasion of their firmness. They walk the road of life, the road fenced in by their tastes, prejudices, disdains or enthusiasms, generally honest, invariably stupid, and are proud of never losing their way. . . . The man of purpose . . . achieves great length without any breadth, and battered, besmirched, and weary, he touches the goal at last; he grasps the reward of his perseverance, of his virtue, of his healthy optimism: an untruthful tombstone over a dark and soon forgotten grave.

(3. ch. 4, p. 197)

Firmness in life, the Dombey-Murdstone firmness, is a kind of self-elected death in life, which receives its confirmation in the tombstone. The man of "purpose" and "firmness" (and we may remind ourselves again that a measure of firmness is necessary to purpose) lives his life in "contempt" for those lost "other human beings" who do not have that firmness. And why, we may ask, is the tombstone "untruthful"? Is it that it is a misrepresentation whether it praise or blame him who lies beneath, a failure to do justice to complexity in the very act of emblematization? As a sign of the better times visited upon Sulaco, Captain Mitchell notes that the equestrian statue has been removed from the square:

There is some talk of replacing it by a marble shaft commemorative of Separation, with angels of peace at the four corners, and bronze Justice holding an even balance, all gilt, at the top.

(*N* 3. ch. 10, p. 482)

One wonders how much conscious artistry went into this, for such signs are indeed, as Melville might have opined, commemorative of separation, of a process of alienation inflicted by the white men on themselves, their women, and the races they exploit. The balance is indeed "all gilt," totally and substantially of the surface, superficial; a balance won, moreover, out of a process that might also inspire the spelling *guilt*. Only Mrs. Gould could have felt that, however.

There is much evidence for suggesting, then, that fetishism and narcissism (and the phallicism that Freud saw to be essential to both) are the central tropes in Conrad's analysis of the colonial experience. The relation of center to circumference, the inner to the outer, so urgently needing to be kept in motion by the Romantic theorists of the mind-world relation, has now become so firmly fixed in an *identity* of inner and outer that redetermination can no longer occur. What might ideally be the challenging of the mind's figures by the world's operations, a process that characterizes Wordsworth's account of the ideal workings of the imagination, has now been replaced by an inert duplication of the one by the other. This is certainly to be related to the white mythology of power, which Marlow fancifully embodies in Jim as "an unthinking and blessed stiffness before the outward and inward terrors" (*LJ*, ch. 5, p. 43). Or at least, that is what Marlow would like to see, because of his own investment in the type. For Jewel, however, this "stiffness" appears as a terrible inhibition on human

exchange: "Ah! you are hard, treacherous, without truth, without com-
passion. What makes you so wicked? Or is it that you are all mad?" (ch. 37,
p. 348).

As the woman's view of Jim is one of uncompromising firmness and
purpose, which we know to be soft, it seems that for other men, and for
Marlow in particular, his image has distinctly feminized overtones. We
hear of his tendency to "blush like a girl" and of his fresh complexion,
"blooming modestly—like a violet" (ch. 18, pp. 195, 187). The winning
qualities of "his hair, his eyes, his smile" (ch. 19, p. 198) make him, for
others, something of a repository of feminine attributes, a figure fulfilling
perhaps some of the fantasies whose analysis Melville had at least suggested in the "handsome sailor" of *Billy Budd* (a story not known to Conrad, but dealing with issues certainly present in other parts of Melville's
work). Here, the rest of Freud's case for the nature of narcissism, which
affects Marlow's perceptions at least as much as it objectively describes
Jim's behavior, offers some worthwhile insights.

Having spoken of the anxiety about "being *watched*" which appears in
the adult narcissist, Freud goes on to relate this to a homosexual libido.
The ego ideal is often imposed by a group (parents, class, nation):

> The want of satisfaction which arises from the non-fulfillment of this ideal
> liberates homosexual libido, and this is transformed into a sense of guilt (social
> anxiety). Originally this sense of guilt was a fear of punishment by the parents,
> or, more correctly, the fear of losing their love; later the parents are replaced by
> an indefinite number of fellow-men.
>
> (*Works* 14. 101–02)

These connections are made very briefly by Freud, and clearly we must
preserve some tact in applying them to Conrad. They do, however, inform
exactly the nature of the relation between Jim, Marlow, and the community of trusted sailors Marlow represents, and sees himself representing. It
is the ideal of seaworthiness that Jim feels that he has betrayed, and it is the
thwarted need to 'belong' which explains both his evasion of publicity in
general, and his particular need to convince Marlow (and of course Marlow's own desire to be convinced) of the community that exists between
them. The "shadowy ideal of conduct" is a mode of self-relation mediated
through the society of upright Englishmen, and that is why it excludes the
"living woman" who has been called Jewel.

That ideal in Jim gravitates toward death, which is both its fulfilment
and its displacement, another version perhaps of the untruthfulness of
tombstones. And, if "full utterance" is indeed the "abiding intention" appearing through and motivating "all our stammerings" (*LJ*, ch. 21, p.
225), then nobody in Conrad's novels seems to achieve it, at least on this
side of the silence of death. Conrad does not provide, at the level either of
language or of metalanguage (that is, either at the level of the novel's
events, in character, or at another level provided by a narrator or author,

from which we may authoritatively judge those events), that "full utterance," which may be read as analogous to the completion that Ishmael had spurned as ethically improper, as promethean madness. The brief snatches of actual dialogue which Marlow records as happening between Jim and himself are models of incompletion and stammering:

> "Thank you, though—your room—jolly convenient—for a chap—badly hipped." . . . The rain pattered and swished in the garden; a water-pipe (it must have had a hole in it) performed just outside the window a parody of blubbering woe with funny sobs and gurgling lamentations, interrupted by jerky spasms of silence. . . . "A bit of shelter," he mumbled and ceased.
>
> (Ch. 16, p. 178)

The passage is exactly as quoted; the spaces dotted to infinity are written in by Conrad. Jim and the water-pipe are companionable forms, to Marlow's mind, as vehicles of disjoined and imperfectly referential sounds. Jim's awkward prep-school patois expresses a greater-than-usual distance—"What a bally ass I've been. . . . You are a brick" (ch. 17, p. 184)—from the kind of discourse that might, if anything could, reestablish a more direct mode of exchange. The absence of such an exchange, mirrored in the narrative in the way in which Jim always has to be hunted for, sought out, commits Marlow yet further to the solipsistic configurations to which he is already all too prone. It prefigures also the drifting off that affects Marlow's own audience at the end of the tale, "as if the last image of that incomplete story, its incompleteness itself, and the very tone of the speaker, had made discussion vain and comment impossible" (ch. 36, p. 337). Moreover, the potential metalanguage is displaced, as Conrad's own vision of Jim's prototype, detailed in the preface, partakes exactly of Marlow's obligation to look from outside, from a position of imposition rather than exchange. Thus Conrad relates: "I saw his form pass by—appealing—significant—under a cloud—perfectly silent" (p. ix). The appeal and the significance depend on silence and on a *seen* form, which cannot reply. In a similar way, all Marlow's predications of significance are founded upon the authority of *seeing*, and that is the one thing that he cannot communicate to his audience through words, trying as he is "to interpret for you into slow speech the instantaneous effect of visual impressions" (ch. 5, p. 48). Conrad in his own voice insists on the same impossible urgency in his preface to *The Nigger of the "Narcissus"*: "before all, to make you *see*" (p. x). The ambiguity deepens, moreover, when Marlow confesses that even the visual confirmation is unsatisfactory; he too is "fated never to see him clearly" (ch. 23, p. 241). In successfully reestablishing the objectivity of optical perception, in fact, Marlow would be turning the whole tide of Romantic speculation, almost as obvious in *Middlemarch* as it is in Blake or Wordsworth, in its emphasis on the figurative status of much so-called 'reality'.

That Marlow cannot do so is crucial, and I think in at least three ways.

First, he cannot put what he sees into words (and, of course, is less than sure of what he sees); second, even if he could, what would be thus communicated might be *his* feelings rather than the person or thing which gave rise to them: "I can't explain to you who haven't seen him and who hear his words only at second hand the mixed nature of my feelings" (ch. 8, p. 93). Is Marlow an innocent eye, and an open heart, so that if he could but communicate efficiently then we could be sure that we were hearing a 'truth'? Does he not have his own motives for seeing Jim the way he does? And third, even if he could turn images and feelings into words, the suggestion is that they might well fall on deaf ears. Saying is not always communicating, and Marlow announces his own cynicism about those who cannot hear his message because their minds are full of other things: "Tomorrow you shall forget my sincerity along with the other lessons of the past" (ch. 13, pp. 152–53); "I could be eloquent were I not afraid you fellows have starved your imaginations to feed your bodies" (ch. 21, p. 255). Marlow himself finds Jim significant. That is why, and because, he "sees" him. The urge to tell is founded on something that would not be what it is if it were not private, or of special significance to idealist sailors.

Thus, even if the lengthy tombstone that is Marlow's narration were to happen to tell the truth, it might not be heard as such. There may be nothing in the society of the audience, Marlow suggests, that would provide a context in which any authentic significance or heroism would register as such. We could go on to infer from this that such a society of listeners is unlikely to *produce* any emissaries capable of heroism, any truly lordly Jims. The tombstone may lie not just about its incumbent, but also about the people who write the epitaphs.

The same insecurity of seeing and telling occurs in *Heart of Darkness*, this time in the image of the dream state. Marlow speaks of

> that Kurtz whom at the time I did not see—you understand. He was just a word for me. I did not see the man in the name any more than you do. Do you see him? Do you see the story? Do you see anything? It seems to me I am trying to tell you a dream. . . .
>
> (Ch. 1, p. 82)

It is in the dream that we both believe and disbelieve the reality of what we see; at least there, perhaps, we can effect the rearrangement of things by association, and free them, perhaps, from a prefigured order. This particular use of the dream image suggests, however, a dissatisfying orbit of disconnected signs. Kurtz is a *name*. Marlow feels something akin to what Wordsworth felt in the city of London, but he feels it everywhere, as much in the sparser regions of central Africa as in the preformed chaos of an urban environment. Marlow seems to see no privileged societies in marginal positions; the possibilities for change seem dampened. The very thing that Wordsworth had so anxiously investigated, the genesis of possible moral and social identities out of the interaction of mind and nature, is squashed by Conrad—and I take it that the pressures are historical—into an immanent similitude.

When Marlow argues for the place of Jim as "one of us" (ch. 35, p. 331)—a phrase Conrad quotes in his own voice in the preface (p. ix)—the community thus implied is one that neither Marlow nor Conrad can assume, unless it is composed of a society of people denied "full utterance" and completion. The consciousness available to Marlow and, whether through him or despite him, to his audience, can thus seem to be a "false consciousness": the phrase is used by Bentham to describe what obtains when a person "believes or imagines certain circumstances to subsist, which in truth do not subsist."[6] Alternatively, and I think more precisely, 'truth' remains what it had been from at least Wordsworth onwards, a viable body of agreed points of reference through which communities enact their relations in ways which their members understand, or at least agree to respect and maintain. Wordsworth certainly understood and experienced the ways in which the deviations of the individual mind and imagination remove it from shared experience and expression. But, if he sees this alienation as (tentatively) socially imposed, he sees it also as radically prophetic and creative of possible new societies, albeit small and marginal ones. The urgency of moral statement remains in Wordsworth's writing; he has not quite given up. In Conrad, however, that hopefulness does not seem to be maintained. The novels provide materials for an analysis of ideology and its effects on the individual and social mind, but they offer us no metalanguage, no sure position from which the *exact* scope and influence of the consolidated figures that constitute ideology may be tested and challenged. This is not a verdict upon Conrad, of course, but an attempt to specify the historical situation of his writings. Wordsworth's alternative societies are marginal enough, but at least they function discursively, however true to life they may or may not have been, *as* alternatives, and however fast he saw them to be disappearing. Conrad, conversely, writes from within an undifferentiated world.

For example, in describing a society in which there are almost no significant women, he by definition cannot say what the world would be if there were. Here is Engels with his own idea of "false consciousness" in a letter to Mehring of 14 July 1893:

> Ideology is a process accomplished by the so-called thinker consciously, it is true, but with a false consciousness. The real motive forces impelling him remain unknown to him; otherwise it simply would not be an ideological process. Hence he imagines false or seeming motive forces. Because it is a process of thought he derives its form as well as its content from pure thought, either his own or that of his predecessors.[7]

By "pure thought" Engels means habitual terms of reference, not referred to anything outside the consciousness. As a proponent both of the necessity and of the inevitability of revolution, Engels must also establish the possibility of metalanguage, an authentic consciousness that can dissipate the false and perceive the true. Conrad is not the proponent of revolution, and his position is harder to plot, if indeed it exists at all as anything other than a strategy of indecision. But this does not disestablish the nature of the analysis that I take his writings to stimulate. Dr. Monygham, for example, explains the situation in Sulaco in terms of which Engels might have approved:

> There is no peace and no rest in the development of material interests. They have their law, and their justice. But it is founded on expediency, and is inhuman; it is without rectitude, without the continuity and the force that can be found only in a moral principle.
>
> (*N* 3. ch. 11, p. 511)

Material interests have infected, and fetishized, the human imagination from within. What Monygham observes here is the social confirmation or perhaps cause of an ethic of highly unenlightened self-interest, as theorized by Schopenhauer and, here, by Bentham:

> Human beings are the most powerful instruments of production, and therefore every one becomes anxious to employ the services of his fellows in multiplying his own comforts. Hence the intense and universal thirst for power; the equally prevalent hatred of subjection. Each man therefore meets with an obstinate resistance to his own will, and is obliged to make an equally constant opposition to that of others, and this naturally engenders antipathy towards the beings who thus baffle and contravene his wishes.
>
> (*Economic Writings* 3. 430)

When self-interest has itself been materialized, then it becomes even more improper, even more of an ignis fatuus. If the will itself is diseased, can there be room for the development of a "moral principle"? Engels might have argued for its possibility in a society outside capital, but there are no such societies in Conrad's novels. Even the ideal alternatives voiced by people like Jim and Marlow are constructed from "within" and are eroded by subtle forms of relation to the corruptions they are trying to displace. There seem to be no pure "militant geographers" left, no unselfish pursuers of mere facts. There are degrees, of course, but although the general context of colonial racism from which Jim is distinguished is appalling, that fact alone does not make Jim a hero of redemptive potential. His own creative drives are also turned into self-consolidation, as he may himself mean to suggest in recognizing the claim upon him posed by Gentleman Brown. One may certainly choose between the *versions* of colonialism, and choose rightly, but this choice remains within the orbit of the interdetermination of trade and imagination. If Marlow appears to the audience of *Heart of Darkness* like an idol, or a Buddha, then there is no way of knowing what a 'pure' perception of Marlow might be. Does he cast himself thus, or is he seen in this way by others, beyond his control?

Even where there is no Marlow, no dramatic narrator, it does not seem that the objectivity of narration thus apparently achieved provides for its readers any secure position from which to judge. Engels again makes an interesting comment in this context. Noting that novels are almost by definition "addressed to readers from bourgeois circles," he writes that

> the socialist problem novel in my opinion fully carries out its mission if by a faithful portrayal of the real conditions it dispels the dominant conventional illusions concerning them, shakes the optimism of the bourgeois world, and inevitably instils doubt as to the eternal validity of that which exists, without itself offering a direct solution of the problem involved, even without at times ostensibly taking sides.[8]

The implication is that the "faithful portrayal of the real" can be written from *within*; it does not require an untainted position outside and beyond implication, outside participation in the very history that is being described. To register confusion or uncertainty is itself to fulfil the demands Engels makes on fictional representation. Conrad certainly seems to meet these requirements as set forth for the "socialist problem novel," regardless of whether or not he would ever have called himself a socialist. The novels offer us materials for making judgments, but they do not unambiguously make them for us—though I hope I have shown that they contain more coherent moral intentions than has often been felt to be the case. The nationalists and populists in *Nostromo* are certainly ridiculed by the omniscient narrator and are never allowed to emerge as a convincing political alternative, but the weight of the analysis in the book is not with them, and it inclines us to think much more seriously about the mine and its worshippers, the apostles of idealized capital. That is the most urgent polemical focus in the writing.

There are no unambiguous positives or easy exits offered by Conrad or by his protagonists in the way of solutions to a predicament of corruption and decline which seems at once psychological and political. That is perhaps appropriate to the voice speaking from 'within.' The famous polemic against the "confounded imagination" (*LJ*, ch. 7, p. 88) appears in Conrad's own voice, as here in the preface to *Victory*: "The habit of profound reflection, I am compelled to say, is the most pernicious of all the habits formed by the civilized man" (pp. x–xi). Similarly, Schopenhauer had seen the man of "genius" as compelled to "eccentricities, personal slips, and even follies" as a result of his experiencing the separation of consciousness from mere willing, with the world thus appearing as an alienated "object of contemplation" instead of remaining an unmediated representation of will (*World as Will and Representation* 2. 387). But this scepticism on Conrad's part about the value of reflective thought does not suggest that the opposite is to be sought, or endorsed when it is found.

When Taminah forgets "the faint and vague image of the ideal" she falls back into the life of the body, an existence marked by "the dreary tranquillity of a desert, where there is peace only because there is no life" (*AF*, ch. 8, p. 116). There is, furthermore, no natural world into which the unconscious human being might be paradisally reclaimed. The creepers of the forest, in searching out the branches of the trees, carry "death to their victims in an exulting riot of silent destruction" (ch. 11, p. 165). The untouched wilderness is nothing more than a "great silence full of struggle and death" (*OI* 5. ch. 2, p. 326). Almayer himself certainly seems to be a product of greed and racial suprematism rather than of any corrupting natural environment, but there seems to be nothing in either man or nature to suggest itself as the basis for an alternative. In the same sense we may contemplate the ambiguities latent in the title *Heart of Darkness*. Part and whole seem to change places, as the map of Africa is the map of the body in what may well be a capitalist geography of narcissism.

For these reasons it is tempting to find a metaphysic, a kind of Schopenhauerian biologism, in Conrad, wherein everything is emptied of moral energy. There is no natural paradise in the wild places of the world, and the human beings inhabiting them are caught in a recurring cycle of frustration, a "monotonous song of praise and desire that, commencing at creation, wraps up the world like an atmosphere and shall end only in the end of all things—when there are no lips to sing and no ears to hear" (*OI* 1. ch. 7, p. 76). The creative interchange possible in Wordsworth because of the partial (but only partial) relation between man and nature is here replaced by a dreary identity. Faced with this, a man like Marlow will admire the assumption of control intimated by even the otherwise most stifling of tailorizations, like the "starched collars and got-up shirt-fronts" of the Company accountant, which call for some respect even if they do make him look like a "hairdresser's dummy" (*HD*, ch. 1, p. 68). Similarly, perhaps, with Mr. Kurtz and the remarkableness of his "lofty frontal bone." But this seems to be an anything better than nothing policy in Marlow. The obsession with parts and attributes which is in Dickens the symptom of a personal or social repression here provides at least something of a relief from the "vision of greyness without form filled with physical pain," and from the terror of having "nothing to say" (ch. 3, p. 151). Similarly, the apparently omniscient narrator who organizes *Nostromo* tells us:

> In our activity alone do we find the sustaining illusion of an independent existence as against the whole scheme of things of which we form a helpless part.
> (3. ch. 10, p. 497)

Such activity, however, has no value, nor does it offer a way of differentiating between various kinds of value, for good and for evil. It is a "sustaining illusion," an efficient figuration allowing us to maintain the performed conviction of an authentic self.

No particular set of sustaining illusions seems to me to have authority in Conrad's novels of empire. Marlow sees in the steamer the "grimy fragment of another world, the forerunner of change, of conquest, of trade, of massacres, of blessings" (*HD*, ch. 3, p. 148). These consequences seem to remain paradoxical for Marlow, and they provide him with the energy for a meditative narration. That is not a position that we need to be satisfied with, but its resolution is a gesture we must enact for ourselves; it is not performed for us. Nor is it possible *not* to resolve. To see the world in a nihilistic frame, and to *try* not to act, is itself paradoxical and inefficient; it is energy devoted to willing itself away. Decoud explains away "all motives and all passions, including his own," but this is no defense against "the darkness of the Placid Gulf" (*N* 2. ch. 8, p. 275). Heyst too is a conscious nihilist: "I shall never lift a little finger again" (*V* 1. ch. 6, p. 54), but Heyst had been born to a father who wrote nihilist aphorisms *instructing* him to "Look on—make no sound" (3. ch. 1, p. 175). He is thus the victim of a double bind; to deny all relation to the world would be to obey the father, but in obeying the father he is accepting relation. Heyst is in this way other to his own otherness, and the alienation is enacted in the images of the father:

> The elder Heyst had written of everything in many books. . . . The son read, shrinking into himself, composing his face as if under the author's eye, with a vivid consciousness of the portrait on his right hand, a little above his head; a wonderful presence in its heavy frame on the flimsy wall of mats, looking exiled and at home, out of place and masterful, in the painted immobility of profile.
> (3. ch. 5, pp. 218–19)

Shrinking, composing, looking up at a presence that is itself mere image, demanding exile and inaction from the son as homage to its own at-homeness of exile. The father's image is integrated in its alienation, most real now when absent and unregainable in death. When Heyst tries to break out of the cycle of obedience to the father by attaching himself to the woman, he can only repeat the act of determination, so that she can say, "It seems to me, somehow, that if you were to stop thinking of me I shouldn't be in the world at all" (3. ch. 3, p. 187). She is renamed by him, a person "to whom, after several experimental essays in combining detached letters and loose syllables, he had given the name of Lena" (p. 186). But this too is secondhand, a working upon the givens. We learn later in the novel that Lena is "the girl they had called Alma—she didn't know why—also Magdalen" (4. ch. 9, p. 367). Heyst's is a merely partial originality, a refiguring of someone else's figure (*-alen* into *Lena*). His movement of difference is compromised from the start by a basis in repetition and inheritance; and none of the names makes sense to the girl they are ostensibly invented to signify. Charms and mysteries are becoming harder to find.

CONCLUSION

"PLOUGHING THE SEA"

The prospect that emerges from this reading of Conrad is one of the alienation of all signifying activity, not only before but also after it has been worked upon by the social or individual imagination. Seeing the world as a series of images no longer produces any positive social bonding, only a galaxy of misdirected energies. Conrad seems to be able to place little faith in the possibilities for any original innocence in perceiving, whether enacted by the young mind or by an adult who has undergone a process of cleansing and moral education. He does not make his protagonists show the *genesis* of alienation so much as its predetermined modulations. There is no moment of pure subjective potentiality from which a falling off might occur, as there is little prospect of a renewed pureness. It is as if the process of duplicating the figurings of a fetishized society now takes place so deep inside the unconscious that it cannot be spoken about, or made the subject of a *drama* whose very energy would suggest the possibility of an alternative. Thus even the nobler gestures of differentiation, like those of Lord Jim, constitute their differences by refining rather than replacing the terms of the prevailing diseases of the imagination. The inscription of a privileged space within which the uncontaminated heart might work for sweetness and light, as it appears in Dickens, albeit with varying and questionable levels of conviction and credibility, seems to disappear altogether in Conrad. The heart, in Dickens, asks to be taken as more than just another way of seeing; it invites allegiance as the first principle in an entirely different social order. Enwrapped as it may be in fictionality, in the 'making things right' aspect of the writer's art, it nevertheless comes into play as an element of text, and as such must be considered. The heart disappears in Conrad, along with the women who are so often in Dickens its vehicle and spirit; or, if it appears, it is as a heart of darkness. If Dombey threatens to deaden the world with his particular form of narcissism and its dependant figures, then there are in the long run exemplary individuals to fight him (though not in time to save Paul Dombey). In Conrad, those who might be thus exemplary, like Edith Travers and Jim, are usually in some way eroded from within by their complicity with what they seem to oppose.

In this way, Conrad has reduced all the potentially dialectical elements in the antithesis of primitive and civilized societies, whereby each might function as an image of what the other is not, to a state of monotonous, undifferentiated oneness. There remain, of course, differences of emphasis, contrasts of the sort made by Nina Almayer between innocent greed and self-interest as typified by the Malays, and the more hypocritical version demonstrated by the whites. There remain elements of a perspective invoked by Müller, as he comments that nothing "puzzles the mere savage more than our restlessness, our anxiety to acquire and to possess, rather than to rest and to enjoy" (*Lectures*, p. 77). For the most part, however, the whole world seems to have been robbed of this potential to enjoy and to have acquired the same restlessness. The fetishized world of the colonial nations has imposed itself upon the far-flung corners of the earth, creating a commerce in the images of its own alienation. Again, Conrad does not tend to show us the genesis of this process of exportation; to do so would be to introduce the energetic antithesis of innocence and corruption which he clearly means to avoid. He does not see things this simply. But we may infer from the world that he does describe that the exportation has taken place and has affected the habits of alternative societies, whether or not they could ever have been described as completely innocent in the first place. Writing strictly within an existing uniformity allows Conrad to avoid determinate speculations about origins.[1]

All this amounts to a denial of 'progress' in the sense in which it was understood by the more confident apostles of European culture. That strong current of faith in the ringing grooves of change and material prosperity was by its very nature in tension with an important element in the Romantic aesthetic whereby, according to Hegel, "the march of mental development is the long and hard struggle to free a content from its sensuous and immediate form, endow it with its appropriate form of thought, and thereby give it simple and adequate expression" (*Philosophy of Right*, p. 139). How, it might be wondered, could the captains of industry enact this move *away from* "sensuous and immediate form" by means of an *increase* in the material resources and capacities of a culture? Dickens and Conrad saw the move to be the other way, towards the production of unpurged images within.

This refusal of the mythology of progress which I take to be central to Conrad's writing is also in tension with the belief in cumulative reason propagated by many of the anthropologists of the later nineteenth century. Fergusson, in accounting for the origins of Buddhism, could describe it as "little more than a revival of the coarser superstitions of the aboriginal races, purified and refined by the application of Aryan morality, and elevated by doctrines borrowed from the intellectual superiority of the Aryan races" (*Tree and Serpent Worship*, p. 62). This is perhaps untypically purple, but we do find everywhere traces of a blind belief in progress out of a condition theorized as original or primitive. M'Lennan, for example, observes that fetishism dies slowly but dies nevertheless, "withdrawing its spirits from one sphere after another on their being brought within the domain of science" (1. p. 423); and Frazer opines piously that "in spite, or perhaps by virtue, of his absurdities man moves steadily upwards; the more we learn of his past history the more groundless does the old theory of his degeneracy prove to be."[2] As time goes on, "morality shifts its ground from the sands of superstition to the rock of reason, from the imaginary to the real, from the supernatural to the natural" (p. 81). Dickens, Melville, and Conrad in their various ways remind us that the real is merely a function of the imaginary that has become more successfully reified.

In Melville and Conrad, however, there yet remains one image that is outside the control of the fetishized imagination and beyond complete conflation with the idols of trade. The sea, in its very emptiness, certainly encourages the imposition of forms and images by the adverting mind. But any narcissism suggested by this is kept away from passage into fetish worship by its formlessness and changefulness, and its flexibility before the interpreting moods of the figuring spirit. Furthermore, with the absence of form, the figures that one person educes from the watery glass do not preclude or determine the uses of the same medium by others.

The sea offers also the prospect of the reassumption of totality and the abolition of difference in a moment of prelapsarian consciousness. It figures us back to a point where choices and priorities, determined as they are by a conviction of difference, are no longer necessary. The energy of self-construction, and of self-projection, is here redundant. Hegel again comes to mind:

> No feeling is so homogeneous with the desire for the infinite, the longing to merge into the infinite, as the desire to immerse one's self in the sea. . . . We are taken away from the world and the world from us. . . . In the sea there is no gap, no restriction, no multiplicity, nothing specific. The feeling of it is the simplest, the least broken up.[3]

With the supersession of the need for choice and the consciousness of difference, there disappear also the problems generated around intention and desire. Subjectivity itself is abolished, as the many become the one. There are no longer body-parts or ornamental attributes to offer themselves as the focus of fetishistic impulses. There is no breaking up. Thus in the "Intimations of Immortality" ode (*Poetical Works* 4. 279–85), Wordsworth projected the "immortal sea" (l. 164) as the image of completion, the repository and synthesizing medium of all created forms, the "Fountains, Meadows, Hills, and Groves" which might potentially forbode a "severing of our loves" (l. 188–89) by virtue of their very particularity.

Ishmael has a similar experience with his hands in a barrel of "sperm," in the "A Squeeze of the Hand" episode of *Moby-Dick* (ch. 94, pp. 526–29). The task of the deckhands is to sort through the vats to liquefy everything "to squeeze the lumps back into fluid" (p. 526). What follows is described as an idyll of integration:

> I almost began to credit the old Paracelsan superstition that sperm is of rare value in allaying the heat of anger: while bathing in that bath, I felt divinely free from all ill-will, or petulance, or malice, of any sort whatsoever.
>
> (P. 527)

Sexual innuendoes aside, this produces a feeling of universal well-being, so that Ishmael wants to appeal to the crew to "squeeze ourselves into each other; let us squeeze ourselves universally into the very milk and sperm of kindness." He goes on, however, to testify to the impossibility of such a fantasy:

> I have perceived that in all cases man must eventually lower, or at least shift, his conceit of attainable felicity; not placing it anywhere in the intellect or the fancy; but in the wife, the heart, the bed, the table, the saddle, the fire-side, the country; now that I have perceived all this, I am ready to squeeze case eternally.
>
> (P. 527)

Life requires the shifting into parts, bed, table, and so forth, and it is indeed only in eternity that everlasting squeezing of case is to be hoped for. To want to avoid lowering and shifting is in fact a death wish (a fact intimated comically here, as it appears more heroically in Ahab's pursuit of the whale), as the account of the calenture tells us. The sailor at the masthead "loses his identity" just as Ishmael wants to do in the vats of sperm; thus it may happen that "you drop through that transparent air into the summer sea, no more to rise for ever. Heed it well, ye Pantheists!" (ch. 35, p. 257).

The prospect or fantasy of a paradisal reintegration, however, persists in life even in the face of a logic that recognizes that its proper place is in death. For "meditation and water are wedded for ever" (ch. 1, p. 94). Narcissus drowned himself (according to Ishmael, if not to the usual version of the myth), enacting the passage to which all such desires subtend:

> But that same image, we ourselves see in all rivers and oceans. It is the image of the ungraspable phantom of life; and this is the key to it all.
>
> (P. 95)

The sea, in its emptiness, promises to contain the "ungraspable"—it conceals (in fantasy) that which, if only it were grasped, would provide completion and full utterance. It conceals whales in general, and Moby-Dick in particular; it conceals also the giant squid, the "unearthly, formless, chance-like apparition of life" (ch. 59, p. 382) which greets the sailors at the exact moment they are expecting the unveiling of the white whale himself, thus fulfilling again the logic of displacement and refusing the aspiration to power implicit in the look. The sea contains the lost object, and the sought substitute; that is, it is *made* or figured to contain them by virtue of its ultimate refusal to reveal. Thus the narrator of *Mardi* comments:

> Though America be discovered, the Cathays of the deep are unknown. And whoso crosses the Pacific might have read lessons to Buffon. The sea-serpent is not a fable; and in the sea, that snake is but a garden worm. There are more wonders than the wonders rejected, and more sights unrevealed than you or I ever dreamt of.
>
> (Ch. 13, p. 39)

In this way the sea is a perfect image for a structure of desire, even as it also threatens to subsume within itself all individuals subject to such aspiration. Its mysteries image the truths man cannot imagine, and its presence is the purifying medium for all his transgressions. Thus Ishmael spurns

> that turnpike earth!—that common highway all over dented with the marks of slavish heels and hoofs; and turned me to admire the magnanimity of the sea which will permit no records.
>
> (Ch. 13, p. 155)

Like whiteness, it permits no intermediate colorings, no writings. The taxonomies and catalogues of *Moby-Dick* stand as testaments to incompletion; the sea is the medium of an inclusion that is also erasure: "in landlessness alone resides the highest truth, shoreless, indefinite as God" (ch. 23, p. 203). This landlessness tempts overexertion or excessive imaginings precisely as an alternative to a self-destroying reflection upon nothingness. Here is the narrator of *Mardi* again, describing the predicament of the becalmed sailor: "To his alarmed fancy, parallels and meridians become emphatically what they are merely designated as being: imaginary lines drawn round the earth's surface. The log assures him that he is in such a place; but the log is a liar; for no place, nor any thing possessed of a local angularity, is to be lighted upon in the watery waste" (ch. 2, pp. 9–10). As far as life goes, Dickens's Mark Tapley, the practical man, tells us, "The sea is as nonsensical a thing as any going. It never knows what to do with itself. It hasn't got no employment for its mind, and is always in a state of vacancy" (*MC*, ch. 15, p. 157). For this very reason, it appeals, in the form of the river, to the distracted personifying mind of Arthur Clennam. After constructing a heavily determining analogy of the landscape with the Meagles family, the one standing for the other, it is the river that offers him relief from the limiting preoccupations of his conscious mind: "So many miles an hour the flowing of the stream, here the rushes, there the lilies, nothing uncertain or unquiet, upon this road that steadily runs away; while you, upon your flowing road of time, are so capricious and distracted" (*LD* 1. ch. 16, p. 121). Consciousness is figurative, and the figures are functions of our obsessions and our needs. When we know they are figures, then they offer also the prospect of disappointment, of their *not* relating to a reality. They commit their inventor to an overindulgence in power which may, as in this case, be itself built upon an underlying help-lessness. Thus it is that Clennam wonders whether "it might be better to flow away monotonously, like the river, and to compound for its insensi-bility to happiness with its insensibility to pain" (p. 127).

What could it be that prevents Clennam from experiencing something creative and exhilarating in the oscillation of joy and pain, each giving way to and defining the other? Shelley put his faith in subversion, enacted by metaphor, as the creative principle in history, and Wordsworth saw the prospect for the education of the imagination in the very inseparability of joy and pain, fear and beauty. Nietzsche too made something positive out of this intuition: "Let us think this thought in its most terrible form: exis-tence as it is, without meaning or aim, yet recurring inevitably without any finale of nothingness: *'the eternal recurrence'* " (*The Will to Power*, p. 35). This terribleness produces a positive energy. In the idea that "morality is itself a form of immorality," contradiction is abolished and "the ho-mogeneity of all events is saved" (p. 172). There is no teleological ideal in nature or in human nature, no far-off divine event. On the contrary, the various species are "in utter disorder, over and against each other" (p. 363). There is no privileged discourse; even rational thought is compulsive in-terpretation, though we do not see it as such (p. 283). And yet Nietzsche is able to accept this radical reconstitution of the human image, able to *joy* in it, as a freedom from good and evil. I think that this can be related—though I am speculating here—to a belief in the *availability* of polymor-phous experience, its reality for the human body. Thus the "wisest man would be the one richest in contradictions" (p. 150), and "plurality of interpretations" is a "sign of strength" (p. 326). Nietzsche comments:

> To *endure* the idea of the recurrence one needs: freedom from morality; new means against the fact of *pain* (pain conceived as a tool, as the father of pleasure; there is no cumulative consciousness of displeasure); the enjoyment of all kinds of uncertainty, experimentalism, as a counterweight to this extreme fatal-ism. . . .
>
> (Pp. 545–46)

There seems to be a faith in a pleasure principle here, to which all pain contributes. Pleasure can always be reapproached out of pain. Thus Hegel speaks of the moment after immersion in water, as man emerges born again: "So soon as the water leaves him, the world around him takes on specific characteristics again, and he comes back strengthened to the con-sciousness of multiplicity" (*Early Theological Writings*, p. 275). Inno-cence follows immersion; what was formerly the stale discord of parts now becomes available for organization into harmony. Hegel, Wordsworth (in this context), and Nietzsche all seem to share a belief in the possibility of a pleasurable return to the figuring of the real, and in the availability of novelty.

Looking to Dickens's writing as a way of explaining Clennam's apparent lack of faith in such an option, we can see a context in which this cyclic interchange of pain and pleasure, each defining the other, does not seem to take place. The exemplary subject can no longer organize the world exactly as she or he might wish to; it has been done already, and it has infected the individual imagination. This relates, though Dickens does not cite such authorities, to those theorists of the division of labor who saw among its effects a *dismembering* of the human psyche and the human body, leaving certain individuals with a subjective identity that is no longer even *capable* of oscillation between antithetical states, if such were ever to become available again.

This is close to the position from which Conrad may be taken to write. Lingard and Edith Travers certainly have the opportunity for significant action and relation, but they are compromised from within by prior socialization. The fluctuation of events in Conrad's novels is not built out of the interaction of different states like joy and pain, but out of the shades and finer degrees of inconsequence and attrition. What might appear, in the abstract, to be an equivalence of opportunity for all people, a free-for-all in which the omnipresence of intention and desire frees us from any concern about authenticity and accountability (one way of reading Nietzsche), is in fact, in Conrad's world, shown to be a struggle of varied interests with different *opportunities* for success. Whites and Malays may share certain features common to something called 'human nature,' but the whites have the greater capacity for destruction and exploitation, and a more coherently developed life-lie to help them carry them out. Similarly men over women. We receive, in this way, something of a double message from Conrad. Here is a passage from the second chapter of *Lord Jim*:

> The *Patna*, with a slight hiss, passed over that plain luminous and smooth, unrolled a black ribbon of smoke across the sky, left behind her on the water a white ribbon of foam that vanished at once, like the phantom of a track drawn upon a lifeless sea by the phantom of a steamer.
>
> (p. 16)

The figuring of 'nonreality' here is complicated, as it had been for Ishmael. The sea does not respond to the inscription of human activities, and the sign of the ship's passage is erased. As such, the sea is frightening and belittling. Marlow speaks later of the tendency of a "boat on the high seas to bring out the Irrational that lurks at the bottom of every thought" (ch. 10, p. 121), and of the rapidity with which the sea avenges the narcissism of our early leanings towards it: "In no other kind of life is the illusion more wide of reality—in no other is the beginning *all* illusion—the disenchantment more swift—the subjugation more complete" (ch. 11, p. 129).

"Ploughing the sea" (*N* 2. ch. 5, p. 187) is Decoud's metaphor for futile activity, and later in the novel its "glittering surface" remains "untroubled by the fall of his body" to its suicide (3. ch. 10, p. 501).

But the doubleness of the message is that the silver in his pockets, like the *Patna*, is real, whatever attributions of unreality they may attract. The sea itself may be pure, and therefore terrifying, as the *surface* over which the vehicles of empire make their way. We have indeed yet to develop the technology to shape that formlessness, though of course we may yet also render it redundant or extinct by the contiguity of other technologies. But if the *Patna* leaves no trace behind it, the ship itself is no phantom. It is a slaver crammed with an illicit cargo run by a crew of ruthless and cowardly racists, and one Jim. Their doings are not rendered positive by the emptiness of the sea, nor is that emptiness made holy by its contrast with the tawdry deeds enacted on its surface. The sea is no longer a source of mystery, as it was in Melville; the relief from constricting or destructive figures is only in death, not in privileged perceptions. There are no elements promising new life, no spaces outside that "merry dance of death and trade" (*HD*, ch. 1, p. 62). In Conrad the sea does not operate as a source and stimulus for continual inquiry, speculation and challenge, as the Protestant consciousness searches for God, the devil, and for itself. It is a mere surface, to be forgotten for as long as possible, to be confronted only at those moments of lapse or crisis when the utilitarian mind cannot keep its threats at bay. It certainly exercises a fascination over the author and his characters, but it does not supply the terms of an infinite fantasy both negative and positive.

The sea, as its depths and mysteries are ignored for the utility of its surface, is being exploited, and the moments of drama in Conrad's sea stories often arise when through some natural process or other, whether storm, typhoon, or calm, it threatens to take its revenge. Hegel had articulated this utilitarian image in a passage that would not seem out of place if spoken by Marlow in one of his more discursive moments:

> The principle of family life is dependence on the soil, on land, *terra firma*. Similarly, the natural element for industry, animating its outward movement, is the sea. Since the passion for gain involves risk, industry though bent on gain yet lifts itself above it; instead of remaining rooted to the soil and the limited circle of civil life with its pleasures and desires, it embraces the element of flux, danger, and destruction. Further, the sea is the greatest means of communication, and trade by sea creates commercial connexions between distant countries and so relations involving contractual rights. At the same time, commerce of this kind is the most potent instrument of culture, and through it trade acquires its significance in the history of the world.
>
> (*Philosophy of Right*, p. 151)

Trade indeed, romantic enough perhaps in a world starved of any alternative romance, is now firmly installed as the model on which the human imagination itself operates in imaging its world. Because of it, and its determination of the available processes of exchange and identification, Conrad's protagonists no longer seem able to *enjoy* the road to dusty (or watery) death. Women and children have disappeared, or are seen to disappear, from the sphere of significant action. Dickens's favorite images of regeneration have been written out of the world, and even restlessness threatens to give way to inertia.

In one way *Moby-Dick* is a Hegelian resummation of history, a playing out in a single fictional work of a whole range of historical and mythological archetypes. In the motley constitution of the ship's crew and in the range of its invocations—the Bible, the Osiris myth, Shakespeare, Milton, Job, Satan, Lear, Prometheus, and so on—the book offers a veritable Noah's ark of human culture and exemplary endeavor. As the *Pequod* is a ship of heroes, so it is simultaneously a ship of fools. All this history, all this energy, is directed by a search for what is concealed and must remain so, and for what has been lost. The white whale both incites and punishes desire, taking vengeance on the avenger whose grief he has caused. He stands as an image of nature's refusal of the process of fetishization. Figured and endowed as he is with man's attributes and man's longings, he claims for himself a *real power* over his worshippers which could never be implemented by mere idols of wood and stone, or mere charms and relics. Dickens's and Conrad's novels show the similarly real power of *inert* fetishes, like money and social identity. Because they are not of nature they are even more terrifying, as they never administer any corrective hints to those trapped into their worship. Moby-Dick in comparison is almost himself heroic, a scourge of God, a warning sign upon his brow for those who can read it. What survives out of this history is not a society educated into ideal community—though of course as readers we may take away our own lessons—but a single orphan, Ishmael, who remains to tell us. But the image of the sea, as it continues to hold from us the white whale and whales in general, is a figure of some promise for future intelligences, and it suggests that there remains at least one principle outside and "below" man which will abolish or prohibit his factional configurations and fictional obsessions. The sinking of the *Pequod* is in this respect something almost cathartic.

In the days of the whaling commissions the ocean no longer suffices for such a purpose. We have developed the figure of space. Conrad wrote before this prospect had become a reality, but it is a moot point whether the romance of exploration and militant geography would have come back upon him invested with any more hopeful canonicals than those evidenced in the "ploughing" of the sea.

NOTES

PREFACE

1. *Lay Sermons*, ed. R. J. White, *The Bollingen Edition of the Collected Works of Samuel Taylor Coleridge*, vol. 6, pp. 79, 30.
2. *Coleridge: Poetical Works*, ed. E. H. Coleridge, p. 240.
3. For a sense of the importance of Puritan theology and its insistence on the recognition of God through His attributes on earth, see Perry Miller, *The New England Mind: The Seventeenth Century*, pp. 10ff.
4. Ian Watt, *Conrad in the Nineteenth Century*, p. 147.
5. For a superb account of Melville's place in a tradition of different and differently motivated readings of Marquesan society, see T. Walter Herbert, Jr., *Marquesan Encounters: Melville and the Meaning of Civilization*.

CHAPTER 1

1. *The Farther Adventures of Robinson Crusoe, &c.* My citations are from *The Shakespeare Head Edition of the Novels and Selected Writings of Daniel Defoe*; here, 3:177.
2. Citations from *Typee* and from *Mardi* are taken from the texts in the Northwestern-Newberry Edition of *The Writings of Herman Melville*, ed. Harrison Hayford, Hershel Parker, and G. Thomas Tanselle; here, ch. 12, p. 91. For *Moby-Dick*, see note 5 to chapter 3.
3. Christoph Meiners, *Allgemeine kritische Geschichte der Religionen*, 1:178, notes that fetishes are open to coercion by their worshippers, and goes on to conjecture that dead animals or animal-parts are more commonly used as fetishes than live ones precisely because they are thus more manipulable, and easier to exercise power over (p. 186). James King, the author of the third part of Cook's *A Voyage to the Pacific Ocean*, noted of the idols of the Sandwich Islanders that "it soon became obvious to us in how little estimation they were held, from their frequent expressions of contempt of them, and from their even offering them to sale for trifles" (3:160).
4. Cook, *A Voyage*, 1:404, observed the same among the Friendly Islanders, but added that they did have "very proper sentiments about the immateriality and immortality of the soul."
5. Sir James G. Frazer, *Totemism and Exogamy*, 4:5.
6. Charles de Brosses, *Du culte des dieux fétiches*, is usually credited with the popularization of the term beyond its specific application to West African cult practices. A notable example of a more specific usage is John Atkins, *A Voyage to Guinea, Brasil, and the West-Indies, in His Majesty's Ships the "Swallow" and "Weymouth."* This includes a comprehensive account of fetishism along the Guinea coast (see especially pp. 79–88), offered in a highly tolerant spirit. Regarding all religions as originally natural, and important only in their capacity for maintaining the social order, Atkins has no condescension or prejudice to overcome, and his observations in many ways anticipate the more systematic conclusions of later anthropologists. The first edition of this book, published in 1735, attracted a lengthy review in *The Present State of the Republick of Letters* 15 (1735):262–78, which concentrates heavily on Atkins's remarks about fetishism. For a good account of de Brosses's seminal little work, see Frank E. Manuel, *The Eighteenth Century Confronts the Gods*, pp. 184–209. Manuel also

finds mention of the Guinean *fetissero* in Bayle and Bekker, and his whole book is valuable for the detailed historical context it provides for the development of an attitude to paganism and idolatry. See also, and especially, his account of Dupuis and of the eighteenth-century interest in phallicism (pp. 259–70), in conjunction with the material of chapter three herein.

7. See my *Wordsworth and the Figurings of the Real*, especially ch. 2.

8. *Novum Organum*, 1:xl–lix, in *The Physical and Metaphysical Works of Lord Bacon*, ed. Joseph Devey, pp. 389–98.

9. *The Friend*, ed. Barbara E. Rooke, *The Bollingen Edition of the Collected Works of Samuel Taylor Coleridge*, vol. 4, 1:490.

10. Immanuel Kant, *Critique of Judgement*, trans. James Creed Meredith, 1:106.

11. William Wordsworth, *The Prelude*, ed. E. de Selincourt, 2:221–24; 8:431–36. These and subsequent citations are from the 1805 text.

12. J.-A. Dulaure, *Histoire abrégée de differens cultes*, 1:27. Translations from French and German are my own except where otherwise stated.

13. For example, *The Works of Thomas Carlyle*, 5:11: "What I called the perplexed jungle of Paganism sprang, we may say, out of many roots: every admiration, adoration of a star or natural object, was a root or fibre of a root; but Hero-worship is the deepest root of all; the tap-root, from which in a great degree all the rest were nourished and grown."

14. F. Max Müller, *Lectures on the Origin and Growth of Religion*, pp. 63–64.

15. Samuel Taylor Coleridge, *Biographia Literaria*, ed. J. Shawcross, 2:16.

16. David Hume, "The Natural History of Religion," in *Essays Moral, Political and Literary*, ed. T. H. Green and T. H. Grose, 2:317. See also idem, *A Treatise of Human Nature*, ed. L. A. Selby-Bigge, pp. 224–25.

17. *The Prose Works of William Wordsworth*, ed. W. J. B. Owen and Jane Worthington Smyser, 3:32.

18. *Home at Grasmere*, ed. Beth Darlington, Ms. B, ll. 687–92 (p. 80).

19. *The Poetical Works of William Wordsworth*, ed. E. de Selincourt, 2:216. I provide a longer account of this poem in *Irony and Authority in Romantic Poetry*, pp. 36–38.

20. Müller was to make the case for contemporaneity in a different way by arguing for fetishism as a derived and decadent rather than an original form of worship, "a parasitical development, intelligible with certain antecedents, but never . . . an original impulse of the human heart" (*Lectures*, p. 117). The Portuguese mariners who coined the term did so, he suggests, because "they themselves were perfectly familiar with a *feitiço* . . . and probably all carried with them some beads, or images, that had been blessed by their priests before they started for their voyage. They themselves were fetish-worshippers in a certain sense" (p. 61).

21. François Marie Arouet de Voltaire, *Philosophical Dictionary*, ed. and trans. Theodore Besterman, p. 244.

22. *Works*, 5:204. Carlyle goes on to argue that everything is clothed in "forms," and because of this he cannot admire the "naked formlessness of Puritanism." But he does recommend its "spirit," and from this he discriminates between *kinds* of forms: "As the briefest definition, one might say, Forms which *grow* round a substance, if we rightly understand that, will correspond to the real nature and purport of it, will be true, good; forms which are consciously *put* round a substance, bad. I invite you to reflect on this. It distinguishes true from false in Ceremonial Form, earnest solemnity from empty pageant, in all human things" (p. 205).

23. *On the Constitution of the Church and State*, ed. John Colmer, *The Bollingen Edition of the Collected Works of Samuel Taylor Coleridge*, vol. 10, p. 121n.

24. John Locke, *Essays on the Law of Nature*, ed. W. von Leyden, p. 261.

25. It is interesting that many of Wordsworth's outcries against the evil effects of outward forms divorced from inner realities are delivered by invoking images of theaters and theatricality. This seems to touch on a Puritan tradition against the theaters which had been going since Shakespeare's time; at least, it is often thus represented.

26. Immanuel Kant, *Religion within the Limits of Reason Alone*, trans. Theodore M. Greene and Hoyt H. Hudson, p. 165.

27. See, for example, *The Friend*, 1:501–2, 505–6, and *Lectures, 1795, on Politics and Religion*, ed. Lewis Patton and Peter Mann, *The Bollingen Edition of the Collected Works of Samuel Taylor Coleridge*, vol. 1, pp. 116–45 *passim*.

28. G. W. F. von Hegel, *Aesthetics: Lectures on Fine Art*, trans. T. M. Knox, p. 321.

29. Compare Kant, *Religion within the Limits of Reason Alone*, p. 180:

> Yet for man the invisible needs to be represented through the visible (the sensuous); yea, what is more, it needs to be accompanied by the visible in the interests of practicability and, though it is intellectual, must be made, as it were (according to a certain analogy), perceptual. This is a means of simply picturing to ourselves our duty in the service of God, a means which, although really indispensable, is extremely liable to the danger of misconstruction; for, through an *illusion* that steals over us, it is easily held to be the *service of God* itself, and is, indeed, commonly thus spoken of.

30. The implications of the poet's avoidance of this position of power is the subject of my *Irony and Authority in Romantic Poetry*.

31. Matthew Arnold, *Culture and Anarchy*, ed. John Dover Wilson, pp. 168, 169, 10. It is worth mentioning that Arnold gave the name "Hebraism" to this fixated respect for a single principle, drawing upon a quite different element in Hebrew theology from that positively invoked by Wordsworth and Hume, its respect for the letter of the law.

32. *The Letters of William and Dorothy Wordsworth: The Early Years, 1787–1805*, ed. E. de Selincourt, p. 684.

33. For Wordsworth on poetic diction, see *Prose Works*, 1:131–33, 160–64; 3:64.

34. [John Gordon, D.D.], *Occasional Thoughts on the Study and Character of Classical Authors, on the Course of Litterature, and the Present Plan of a Learned Education, with Some Incidental Comparisons between Homer and Ossian*, p. 38.

35. William Godwin, *Enquiry concerning Political Justice and Its Influence on Morals and Happiness*, corrected and ed. F. E. L. Priestley, 2:102.

36. 3:307–28. I give a reading of this passage in *Wordsworth and the Figurings of the Real*, pp. 49–52.

37. Adam Ferguson, *An Essay on the History of Civil Society*, ed. Duncan Forbes, p. 252.

38. For another of Wordsworth's attempts to negotiate a 'middle ground' between nature and culture in the business of mansions, see *Letters: The Early Years*, p. 625.

39. C. F. Dupuis, *Origine de tous les cultes, ou réligion universelle*, 3:615. Compare Blake's account, in "The Marriage of Heaven and Hell," of the origin of priesthood:

> The ancient Poets animated all sensible objects with Gods or Geniuses, calling them by the names and adorning them with the properties of woods, rivers, mountains, lakes, cities, nations, and whatever their enlarged & numerous senses could percieve.
>
> And particularly they studied the genius of each city & country. placing it under its mental deity.
>
> Till a system was formed, which some took advantage of & enslav'd the vulgar by attempting to realize or abstract the mental deities from their objects; thus began Priesthood:
>> Choosing forms of worship from poetic tales.
>> And at length they pronouncd that the Gods had orderd such things.
>> Thus men forgot that All deities reside in the human breast.

See *The Poetry and Prose of William Blake*, ed. David V. Erdman, p. 37.

40. Karl Marx, *Capital*, vol. 1, trans. Ben Fowkes, p. 149n.

41. G. W. F. von Hegel, *Phenomenology of Spirit*, trans. A. V. Miller, p. 311.

42. *The Theory of Moral Sentiments*, ed. D. D. Raphael and A. L. Macfie, *The Glasgow Edition of the Works and Correspondence of Adam Smith*, vol. 1, pp. 61–62, 63.

43. *An Inquiry into the Nature and Causes of the Wealth of Nations*, ed. R. H. Campbell, A. S. Skinner, and W. B. Todd, *The Glasgow Edition of the Works and Correspondence of Adam Smith*, vol. 2, p. 349. In this context there is a further account of Smith in *Wordsworth and the Figurings of the Real*, pp. 156–59.

44. Again, there is a short account of the arguments about luxury in *Wordsworth and the Figurings of the Real*, pp. 159–61.

45. Jean Jacques Rousseau, *"The Social Contract" and "Discourses,"* trans. G. D. H. Cole, p. 227.

46. Lewis de Bougainville, *A Voyage Round the World, Performed by the Order of His Most Christian Majesty, in the Years 1766, 1767, 1768, and 1769*, trans. John Reinhold Forster, p. 360.

47. Karl Marx and Friedrich Engels, *Collected Works*, 3:212.

48. The phrase is Samuel Johnson's and appears in the "Life of Cowley"; see *Johnson: Poetry and Prose*, ed. Mona Wilson, p. 798.

49. [John Brown], *An Estimate of the Manners and Principles of the Times*, 1:155. The comparison of the passion for money with the natural passions is interesting as an anticipation of what Steven Marcus has convincingly analyzed as the superimposition of economic metaphors upon bodily processes in nineteenth-century discourse. See *The Other Victorians: A Study of Sexuality and Pornography in Mid-Nineteenth-Century England*, especially pp. 21ff.

50. *Jeremy Bentham's Economic Writings*, ed. W. Stark, 3:438.

CHAPTER 2

1. J. C. F. von Schiller, *On the Aesthetic Education of Man*, trans. Elizabeth M. Wilkinson and L. A. Willoughby, p. 33.

2. *Oliver Twist*, ed. Kathleen Tillotson, ch. 37, p. 239. Brackets indicate a manuscript passage.

3. Marshall Berman, *The Politics of Authenticity: Radical Individualism and the Emergence of Modern Society*, see especially pp. xxi, 19.

4. With the exceptions of *Oliver Twist* (see note 2) and *Dombey and Son* (see note 5), quotes are from *The Charles Dickens Edition*, giving abbreviated titles and chapter and page numbers. Here, *LD*, 1. ch. 13, p. 94.

5. *Dombey and Son*, ed. Alan Horsman, ch. 47, p. 619.

6. Max Byrd, *London Transformed: Images of the City in the Eighteenth Century.*

7. Tobias Smollett, *The Expedition of Humphry Clinker*, ed. Lewis M. Knapp, p. 90.

8. Charlotte Brontë, *Jane Eyre*, ed. Jane Jack and Margaret Smith, pt. 2, ch. 9, p. 339. Jane herself is not averse to such games, nor obviously out of control of the consequences; but she does say, later: "I could not, in those days, see God for his creature; of whom I had made an idol" (p. 346).

9. *Hegel's Philosophy of Right*, trans. T. M. Knox, p. 145.

10. A point made by J. Hillis Miller in his introduction to the Penguin edition of *Bleak House*, p. 22.

11. Again, Marcus's argument in *The Other Victorians: A Study of Sexuality and Pornography in Mid-Nineteenth-Century England*, comes to mind as a way of contributing to an explanation of the extremes of maleness presented in Dickens. Particularly important is the account (pp. 25ff.) of the "double bind" whereby all *expense* of semen, whether in lawful or unlawful sexual relations or in masturbation, is a *waste*, a depletion of *resources* that might otherwise be directed outwards, towards some chosen image of the self, or some version of cultural architecture. By analogy, Dickens's hapless males look like spenders, as his aggressive ones are savers, with an excess of capital energy to discharge elsewhere.

12. Arthur Schopenhauer, *The World as Will and Representation*, trans. E. F. J. Payne, 2:381.

CHAPTER 3

1. James Fergusson, *Tree and Serpent Worship: Or Illustrations of Mythology and Art in India in the First and Fourth Centuries after Christ, from the Sculptures of the Buddhist Topes at Sanchi and Amravati*, p. 1.

2. J. F. M'Lennan, "The Worship of Animals and Plants," *The Fortnightly Review*; pt. 1, "Totems and Totemism," n.s. 6 (1869): 407–27; pt. 2, "Totem Gods among the Ancients," n.s. 7 (1870): 194–216.

3. Rather less anthropological is Mrs. J. H. Philpot's *The Sacred Tree; Or, the Tree in Religion and Myth*. But, though recognizing that the tree may appear as "the symbol and minister of fecundity" (p. 76), the author is careful to avoid any explicit analysis of phallicism.

4. *OED* suggests that the primary senses of *erect* invoked in Godwin's passage, those of "not downcast, unabashed," and perhaps "alert, attentive," were contemporaneous with the physiological reading hinted at (by transference, of course, to the "front") by the contiguity of the word *emasculated*. This word too had a common derived meaning, "unmanly, effeminate," and to say that Godwin intends any direct sexual reference is of course interpretative on my part. However, images of firmness and uprightness are commonplace in the eighteenth-century rhetoric of civic virtue, as their opposites accompany the onset of tyranny and luxury. Locke, in his attack on the patriarchal apologia of Filmer in the *Two Treatises of Government* (ed. Peter Laslett), had ridiculed the idea of the king as a tyrant father over his subjects, "so that he may take or alienate their Estates, sell, castrate, or use their Persons as he pleases, they being all his Slaves, and he Lord or Proprietor of every Thing, and his unbounded Will their Law" (1. ch. 2, sect. 9, p. 166).

5. Harold Beaver's notes to his edition of the novel (Harmondsworth, Middlesex: Penguin Books, 1972) provide an excellent reference point for all of the obvious, and some of the not so obvious, phallic allusions in the book. The textual history of *Moby-Dick* is rather complicated. I have quoted from Beaver's edition throughout, but the reader may assume that I have in all cases checked citations against the most widely used standard edition, that of Harrison Hayford and Hershel Parker. For an account of the textual predicament, see Beaver, pp. 43–60, and Hayford and Parker, pp. 471–98. As it happens, in the passages I have cited there are no meaningful discrepancies between the first English and first American editions. In my account of *Moby-Dick* I have learned, as so many readers must have, from Charles Feidelson Jr.'s *Symbolism and American Literature*, and also from James Guetti, *The Limits of Metaphor: A Study of Melville, Conrad, and Faulkner*.

6. *Buffon's Natural History* notes that ambergris was at first thought to be a substance floating on the surface of the sea: "but time, that reveals the secrets of the mercenary, has discovered that it chiefly belongs to this animal. The name, which has been improperly given to the former substance [spermaceti], seems more justly to belong to this; for the ambergrise is found in the place where the seminal vessels are usually situated in other animals" (2. 11). The same passage appears word for word in *A History of the Earth and Animated Nature*, by Oliver Goldsmith, 3:423.

7. Friedrich Nietzsche, *The Will to Power*, trans. Walter Kaufmann and R. J. Hollingdale, p. 3.

8. The narrator of *Mardi* comments on the "horrific serenity of aspect" of the white shark (ch. 13, p. 41), which both terrifies and mesmerizes him.

9. *Goethe's Theory of Colours*, trans. Charles Lock Eastlake, pp. 6, 7.

CHAPTER 4

1. I quote from *The Works of Joseph Conrad*, The Uniform Edition, giving abbreviated titles and chapter numbers. Thus, in this instance, *AF*, ch. 1, p. 3.

2. Joseph Conrad, *Last Essays*, p. 14.

3. Compare Karl Marx, *Capital*, vol. 1, trans. Ben Fowkes: "This physical object, gold or silver in its crude state, becomes, immediately on its emergence from the bowels of the earth, the direct incarnation of all human labour. Hence the magic of money. Men are henceforth related to each other in their social process of production in a purely atomistic way. Their own relations of production therefore assume a material shape which is independent of their control and their conscious individual action" (p. 187).

4. *The Standard Edition of the Complete Psychoanalytical Works of Sigmund Freud*, ed. James Strachey and Anna Freud, 7:171. The point had been anticipated by Alfred Binet, in his paper "Le fétichisme dans l'amour," pp. 1–85, in *Études de psychologie experimentale*. Binet comments that "everyone is more or less fetishistic in love" (p. 4), and that fetishism exists as an element in normal love relations: "it only takes the seed to germinate for the perversion to appear" (p. 82). My translations.

5. Those parts of Freud's argument most central to Jim's case are in fact anticipated by Binet. Binet does not relate fetishism specifically, or indeed at all, to phallicism, but he does note that it may be focused on psychic as well as on material attributes ("Le fétichisme," p. 57); that it tends to produce continence—as it did in Rousseau (p. 53)—and cannot entail conventional reproduction, given that the fetishist loves "an object or a fraction of the living person" (p. 75); and that it attracts to itself all perceptual and relational energies by association, thus effecting a "considerable modification of the character and personality of the individual" (p. 15). Particularly interesting, in terms of my case for the historical identity of and concern with fetishism, and its place in the Romantic and nineteenth-century debate about the figurative, is this passage at the end of Binet's account:

> Normal love thus appears to us as the result of a complicated fetishism; one could say—and I employ this comparison only to make the thought precise—that in normal love fetishism is polytheistic. It results, not in a single excitation, but in a host of them; it is a symphony. Where does the pathology begin? It appears at the moment when the love of a particular detail becomes preponderant, eliminating all the rest.
>
> Normal love is a harmony. The lover loves to the same degree all the elements in the woman he loves, all the parts of her body and all the manifestations of her spirit. In sexual perversion, we do not see anything new happen; it is simply that the harmony is broken, and love, instead of being excited by the whole person, is now excited only by a part. Here, the part substitutes for the whole, the attribute becomes the quality. Monotheism answers polytheism. The love of the pervert is a piece of theatre wherein a mere extra comes to the apron and usurps the leading rôle.

(pp. 84–85)

Thus is the interplay of the many and the one disrupted by the claim of the fetish.

6. Jeremy Bentham, *An Introduction to the Principles of Morals and Legislation*, p. 71.

7. Karl Marx and Friedrich Engels, *Selected Works*, 3:496.

8. *Marx, Engels: On Literature and Art*, p. 88.

CONCLUSION

1. In one version of the economic cycle, the 'fetishization' of a civilized state is a consequence of the same conditions that oblige it to seek colonial territories and markets. Divided labor within a society produces a surplus that must be disposed of overseas, as it more than meets national demands; see *Hegel's Philosophy of Right*, trans. T. M. Knox, pp. 150–51.

2. Sir James G. Frazer, *Psyche's Task: A Discourse concerning the Influence of Superstition on the Growth of Institutions*, p. vii.

3. G. W. F. von Hegel, *Early Theological Writings*, trans. T. M. Knox, p. 275.

BIBLIOGRAPHY

Arnold, Matthew. *Culture and Anarchy*. Edited by John Dover Wilson. Corrected edition. Cambridge: Cambridge University Press, 1935.

Atkins, John. *A Voyage to Guinea, Brasil, and the West-Indies, in His Majesty's Ships the "Swallow" and "Weymouth."* 2d ed. London, 1737.

Bacon, Francis. *The Physical and Metaphysical Works of Lord Bacon*. Edited by Joseph Devey. London: Henry Bohn, 1858.

Bentham, Jeremy. *An Introduction to the Principles of Morals and Legislation*. New York: Hafner Publishing Co., 1948.

————. *Jeremy Bentham's Economic Writings*. Edited by W. Stark. 3 vols. London: George Allen & Unwin for the Royal Economic Society, 1952.

Berman, Marshall. *The Politics of Authenticity: Radical Individualism and the Emergence of Modern Society*. London: George Allen & Unwin, 1970.

Binet, Alfred. "Le fétichisme dans l'amour." In *Études de psychologie experimentale*, pp. 1–85. Paris: Octave Doin, 1888.

Blake, William. *The Poetry and Prose of William Blake*. Edited by David V. Erdman, commentary by Harold Bloom. 4th printing, with revisions. Garden City, N.Y.: Doubleday & Co., 1970.

Bougainville, Lewis de. *A Voyage Round the World, Performed by the Order of His Most Christian Majesty, in the Years 1766, 1767, 1768, and 1769*. Translated by John Reinhold Forster. London, 1772.

Brontë, Charlotte. *Jane Eyre*. Edited by Jane Jack and Margaret Smith. The Clarendon Edition of the Novels of the Brontës. Reprint, with corrections. Oxford: Clarendon Press, 1974.

[Brosses, Charles de.] *Du culte des dieux fétiches*. Paris, 1760.

[Brown, John.] *An Estimate of the Manners and Principles of the Times*. 2 vols. London, 1757 and 1758.

Buffon, George Louis Leclerc, Comte de. *Buffon's Natural History*. Abridged. 2 vols. Berwick, 1807.

Byrd, Max. *London Transformed: Images of the City in the Eighteenth Century*. New Haven: Yale University Press, 1978.

Carlyle, Thomas. *The Works of Thomas Carlyle*. The Centenary Edition. 30 vols. London: Chapman & Hall, 1896–99.

Coleridge, Samuel Taylor. *Biographia Literaria*. Edited by J. Shawcross. Reprinted, with corrections. 2 vols. London: Oxford University Press, 1954.

————. *Coleridge: Poetical Works*. Edited by E. H. Coleridge. London: Oxford University Press, 1969.

————. *The Bollingen Edition of the Collected Works of Samuel Taylor Coleridge*. Edited by Kathleen Coburn, with Bart Winer. 16 vols., in progress. London: Routledge & Kegan Paul; Princeton: Princeton University Press, 1969–. Vol. 4. *The Friend*. Edited by Barbara E. Rooke. 2 vols. 1969. Vol. 1. *Lectures,*

1795, on Politics and Religion. Edited by Lewis Patton and Peter Mann, 1971. Vol. 6. *Lay Sermons.* Edited by R. J. White, 1972. Vol. 10. *On the Constitution of the Church and State.* Edited by John Colmer, 1976.

Conrad, Joseph. *The Works of Joseph Conrad.* The Uniform Edition. 22 vols. London: J. M. Dent & Sons, 1923–28.

―――. *Last Essays.* London: J. M. Dent & Sons, 1926.

Cook, James. *A Voyage to the Pacific Ocean, Undertaken by the Command of His Majesty, for Making Discoveries in the Northern Hemisphere, to Determine the Position and Extent of the West Side of North America; And the Practicability of a Northern Passage to Europe. Performed under the Direction of Captains Cook, Clerke, and Gore, in His Majesty's Ships the RESOLUTION and DISCOVERY; in the Years 1776, 1777, 1778, 1779, and 1780.* 3 vols. Vols. 1 and 2 by James Cook. Vol. 3 by James King. London, 1784.

Defoe, Daniel. *The Shakespeare Head Edition of the Novels and Selected Writings of Daniel Defoe.* 14 vols. Oxford: Basil Blackwell, 1927–28.

Dickens, Charles. *The Charles Dickens Edition.* 18 vols. London: Chapman & Hall, 1867–74.

―――. *Oliver Twist.* Edited by Kathleen Tillotson. The Clarendon Dickens. Oxford: Clarendon Press, 1966.

―――. *Bleak House.* Edited by J. Hillis Miller. Harmondsworth, Middlesex: Penguin Books, 1971.

―――. *Dombey and Son.* Edited by Alan Horsman. The Clarendon Dickens. Oxford: Clarendon Press, 1974.

Dulaure, J.-A. *Histoire abrégée de differens cultes.* 2d ed. 2 vols. Paris, 1825.

Dupuis, C. F. *Origine de tous les cultes, ou réligion universelle.* 7 vols. Paris, 1822.

Engels, Friedrich. See Marx, Karl.

Feidelson, Charles, Jr. *Symbolism and American Literature.* Chicago: University of Chicago Press, 1953.

Ferguson, Adam. *An Essay on the History of Civil Society.* Edited by Duncan Forbes. Edinburgh: Edinburgh University Press, 1966.

Fergusson, James. *Tree and Serpent Worship: Or Illustrations of Mythology and Art in India in the First and Fourth Centuries after Christ, from the Sculptures of the Buddhist Topes at Sanchi and Amravati.* London, 1868.

Frazer, Sir James G. *Psyche's Task: A Discourse concerning the Influence of Superstition on the Growth of Institutions.* London: Macmillan, 1909.

―――. *Totemism and Exogamy.* 4 vols. London: Macmillan, 1910.

Freud, Sigmund. *The Standard Edition of the Complete Psychoanalytical Works of Sigmund Freud.* Edited by James Strachey and Anna Freud. 24 vols. London: Hogarth Press, 1953–66.

Godwin, William. *Enquiry concerning Political Justice and Its Influence on Morals and Happiness.* Facsimile of the 3d ed., with corrections. Edited F. E. L. Priestley. 3 vols. Toronto: University of Toronto Press, 1946.

Goethe, J. W. von. *Goethe's Theory of Colours.* Translated by Charles Lock Eastlake. 1840. Reprint. London: Frank Cass & Co., 1967.

Goldsmith, Oliver. *A History of the Earth and Animated Nature.* 4 vols. Ormskirk, 1807.

[Gordon, John, D. D.] *Occasional Thoughts on the Study and Character of Classi-*

cal Authors, on the Course of Litterature, and the Present Plan of a Learned Education, with Some Incidental Comparisons between Homer and Ossian. London, 1762.

Guetti, James. *The Limits of Metaphor: A Study of Melville, Conrad, and Faulkner.* Ithaca: Cornell University Press, 1967.

Hartman, Geoffrey H. *Wordsworth's Poetry, 1787–1814.* New Haven: Yale University Press, 1964.

Hegel, G. W. F. von. *Early Theological Writings.* Translated by T. M. Knox. 1948. Reprint. Philadelphia: University of Pennsylvania Press, 1971.

————. *Hegel's Philosophy of Right.* Translated by T. M. Knox, 1952. Reprint. Oxford: Oxford University Press, 1975.

————. *Aesthetics: Lectures on Fine Art.* Translated by T. M. Knox. 2 vols. Oxford: Clarendon Press, 1975.

————. *Phenomenology of Spirit.* Translated by A. V. Miller. Oxford: Clarendon Press, 1977.

Herbert, T. Walter, Jr. *Marquesan Encounters: Melville and the Meaning of Civilization.* Cambridge: Harvard University Press, 1980.

Hume, David. "The Natural History of Religion." In *Essays Moral, Political and Literary,* edited by T. H. Green and T. H. Grose. 2 vols. London: Longman's, Green & Co., 1875.

————. *A Treatise of Human Nature.* Edited by L. A. Selby-Bigge. 1888. Reprint. Oxford: Clarendon Press, 1973.

Johnson, Samuel. *Johnson: Prose and Poetry.* Edited by Mona Wilson. 2d ed. London: Rupert Hart-Davis, 1957.

Kant, Immanuel. *Critique of Judgement.* Translated by James Creed Meredith. 2 vols. in 1. 1928. Reprint. Oxford: Clarendon Press, 1952, 1973.

————. *Religion within the Limits of Reason Alone.* Translated by Theodore M. Greene and Hoyt H. Hudson. 1934. Reprint. New York: Harper & Row, 1960.

King, James. See Cook, James.

Knight, Richard Payne. *An Inquiry into the Symbolical Language of Ancient Art and Mythology.* London, 1818.

Locke, John. *Essays on the Law of Nature.* Edited by W. von Leyden. Oxford: Clarendon Press, 1954.

————. *Two Treatises of Government.* Edited by Peter Laslett. Cambridge: Cambridge University Press, 1960.

M'Lennan, J. F. "The Worship of Animals and Plants." Pt. 1. "Totems and Totemism." *The Fortnightly Review,* n.s. 6 (1869): 407–27. Pt. 2. "Totem Gods among the Ancients." *The Fortnightly Review,* n.s. 7 (1870): 194–216.

Manuel, Frank E. *The Eighteenth Century Confronts the Gods.* Cambridge: Harvard University Press, 1959.

Marcus, Steven. *The Other Victorians: A Study of Sexuality and Pornography in Mid-Nineteenth-Century England.* London: Weidenfeld & Nicolson, 1966.

Marx, Karl. *Capital.* Vol. 1. Translated by Ben Fowkes. New York: Random House, 1977.

Marx, Karl, and Engels, Friedrich. *Selected Works.* 3 vols. Moscow: Progress Publishers, 1970.

————. *Collected Works.* In progress. London: Lawrence & Wishart, 1975–.

————. *Marx, Engels: On Literature and Art*. Moscow: Progress Publishers, 1976.

Meiners, Christoph. *Allgemeine kritische Geschichte der Religionen*. 2 vols. Hannover, 1806–07.

Melville, Herman. *Moby-Dick*. Edited by Harrison Hayford and Hershel Parker. New York: W. W. Norton & Co., 1967.

————. *Moby-Dick*. Edited by Harold Beaver. Harmondsworth, Middlesex: Penguin Books, 1972.

————. *The Writings of Herman Melville*. The Northwestern-Newberry Edition. Edited by Harrison Hayford, Hershel Parker and G. Thomas Tanselle. In progress. Evanston: Northwestern University Press; Chicago: The Newberry Library, 1968–.

Miller, Perry. *The New England Mind: The Seventeenth Century*. 1939. Reprint. Boston: Beacon Press, 1961.

Müller, F. Max. *Lectures on the Origin and Growth of Religion*. London: Longmans, Green & Co., 1878.

Nietzsche, Friedrich. *The Will to Power*. Translated by Walter Kaufmann and R. J. Hollingdale. New York: Randon House, 1968.

Payne Knight. See Knight, Richard Payne.

Philpot, Mrs. J. H. *The Sacred Tree; Or, the Tree in Religion and Myth*. London: Macmillan, 1897.

Review of John Atkins, *A Voyage to Guinea, Brasil, and the West-Indies, in His Majesty's Ships the "Swallow" and "Weymouth,"* in *The Present State of the Republick of Letters* 15 (1735): 262–78.

Rousseau, Jean Jacques. *"The Social Contract" and "Discourses."* Translated by G. D. H. Cole. 1913. Reprint. London: Dent & Dutton, 1963.

Schiller, J. C. F. von. *On the Aesthetic Education of Man*. Translated by Elizabeth M. Wilkinson and L. A. Willoughby. Oxford: Clarendon Press, 1967.

Schopenhauer, Arthur. *The World as Will and Representation*. Translated by E. F. J. Payne. 2 vols. 1958. Reprint. New York: Dover Publications, 1966.

Simpson, David. *Irony and Authority in Romantic Poetry*. London: Macmillan, 1979.

————. *Wordsworth and the Figurings of the Real*. London: Macmillan, 1982.

Smith, Adam. *The Glasgow Edition of the Works and Correspondence of Adam Smith*. In progress. Oxford: Clarendon Press, 1976–. Vol. 1. *The Theory of Moral Sentiments*. Edited by D. D. Raphael and A. L. Macfie. 1976. Vol. 2. *An Inquiry into the Nature and Causes of the Wealth of Nations*. Edited by R. H. Campbell, A. S. Skinner, and W. B. Todd. 2 vols. 1976.

Smollett, Tobias. *The Expedition of Humphry Clinker*. Edited by Lewis M. Knapp. Oxford English Novels. London: Oxford University Press, 1966.

Voltaire, François Marie Arouet de. *Philosophical Dictionary*. Edited and translated by Theodore Besterman. 1971. Reprint. Harmondsworth, Middlesex: Penguin Books, 1979.

Watt, Ian. *Conrad in the Nineteenth Century*. Berkeley and Los Angeles: University of California Press, 1979.

Wordsworth, William. *The Poetical Works of William Wordsworth*. Edited by E. de Selincourt. 5 vols. Oxford: Clarendon Press, 1940–49.

————. *The Prelude*. Edited by E. de Selincourt. 2d ed. Revised by Helen Darbishire. Oxford: Clarendon Press, 1959.

_____. *The Letters of William and Dorothy Wordsworth: The Early Years, 1787–1805*. Edited by E. de Selincourt. 2d ed. Revised by Chester L. Shaver. Oxford: Clarendon Press, 1967.

_____. *The Prose Works of William Wordsworth*. Edited by W. J. B. Owen and Jane Worthington Smyser. 3 vols. Oxford: Clarendon Press, 1974.

_____. *Home at Grasmere*. Edited by Beth Darlington. The Cornell Wordsworth. Ithaca, N.Y.: Cornell University Press; Hassocks, Sussex: Harvester Press, 1977.

INDEX

Arnold, Matthew, 20, 58, 129
Atkins, John, 45, 74, 127
Austen, Jane, 47, 56

Bacon, Francis, 10, 46, 91; Coleridge on, 11
Bentham, Jeremy, 37, 112, 113
Berman, Marshall, 44, 46
Binet, Alfred, 132
Blake, William, 95, 129
Brontë, Charlotte, 49, 54, 56, 130
Brown, John, 36, 47
Buffon, George Louis Leclerc, Comte de, 131
Byrd, Max, 46

Carlyle, Thomas: and Dickens, 42–44; on fetishism, 20, 42–44; and Godwin, 43–44; on hero worship, 128; on money, 33; on Puritanism, 17, 128; *Sartor Resartus*, 42–44; on trade, 69–71; and Wordsworth, 43
Catholicism, and idolatry, 17–18
City and country, xii–xiii, 46–47
Clothing, 40–46, 71–72. *See also* Ornament
Coleridge, Samuel Taylor: on clerisy, 11; and Dickens, 42, 48; on fetishism, 20; on the Hebrews, 18; on idolatry, 11–13; on imagination, 34, 86; on "symbol," xiii, 19, 42, 48
Commerce and technology: Carlyle on, 69–71; Conrad on, 95–107, 118–19, 124–26; Hegel on, 132; and imagination, 93–116, 118–19, 124–26; Müller on, 119; Smith on, 95; in whaling industry, 82–83, 92–94
Commodity, 30–38, 95–97, 102; Marx on, 32–35, 37, 41, 132; Smith on, 30–31, 35–36
Conrad, Joseph, xiv–xvi, xviii, 8, 30, 81, 92–116, 117–26 passim; alienation of the sexes in, 72–73, 95–116, 118, 124–26; commerce and imagination in, 95–107, 118–19, 124–26; and homosexuality, 109–11; on idolatry, 105–8; Marlow, character of, 97–99, 102–3, 105–7, 109–12;

and Melville, 70–73, 109; and narcissism, 73, 95, 102–10, 120, 124–25; and phallicism, 95, 106; and 'progress,' 118–20; on racism, 98–116, 119, 124; on the sea, 120, 124–26; and Wordsworth, 112. Works: *Almayer's Folly*, 95, 97, 99, 101, 115; "Geography and Some Explorers," 99; *Heart of Darkness*, 97–99, 106–7, 111, 113–16, 125; *Karain*, 101–2; *Lord Jim*, 97–98, 100, 102–5, 107–11, 113, 114, 118, 124–25; *Nigger of the 'Narcissus,'* 110; *Nostromo*, 96–97, 100–101, 105–6, 108, 113–16, 125; *An Outcast of the Islands*, 97–99, 101, 105, 107, 115; *The Rescue*, 104–5, 124; *Victory*, 98, 107, 114, 116
Cook, James, 29, 74, 127
Cooper, James Fenimore, 85
Cuvier, Frederick, vii, xi,

de Bougainville, Lewis, 29–30
de Brosses, Charles, 13–14, 16, 37–38, 127
Defoe, Daniel, 4–9, 17, 74
Dickens, Charles: adult-child relations in, 57–60; authority in, 62–63, 118; and Carlyle, 42–44; character in, 40–42; and Coleridge, 48; comedy in, 47–48; family in, 53–55, 62, 72, 95; fetishism in, xiv, 11, 20, 46–68, 118; figurative mode in, 46–68, 118, 124; male-female relations in, 56–57, 60–62, 130; mastery and slavery in, 92–93; and Melville, 70; metaphor in, 66, 94–95; metonymy in, 66; money in, 60–61; names in, 27, 52–55; pathetic fallacy, use of, 63–68; phallicism in, xiv, 59–62, 75; the sea in, 122–23; and Wordsworth, 41. Works: *Barnaby Rudge*, 54, 57; *Bleak House*, 47, 50, 52, 53, 56–59, 75; *David Copperfield*, 48, 53–59, 61–62, 67–68; *Dombey and Son*, 32, 45–46, 48–50, 52–54, 56, 58–61, 64, 75, 92, 98, 118; *Great Expectations*, 51–54, 56, 58; *Hard Times*, 47, 49, 55, 59, 65–66, 94–95; *Little Dorrit*, 45, 47–51, 53, 56–57, 63, 66, 122-23; *Martin Chuzzlewit*, 53, 56; *Nicholas Nickleby*, 48-49, 51, 53, 57;

Phallicism: in Conrad, 95, 106–9; in Defoe, 5, 74; in Dickens, xiv, 59–62, 75; Dulaure on, 73–74, 106; and fetishism, 73–75, 128; and Godwin, 131; Meiners on, 74; in Melville, xiv, 6, 73–90; and metonymy, 73
Philpot, Mrs. J. H., 131

Rousseau, Jean Jacques, 28, 30, 44–45, 46, 71

Schiller, J. C. F. von, 42, 86
Schopenhauer, Arthur, 64, 113, 114
Sea, image of the, 120–26; Conrad on, 120, 124–26; Dickens on, 122–23; Hegel on, 120, 123–24, 125; Melville on, 121–22; Wordsworth on, 120
Shelley, Percy Bysshe, 31, 64, 123
Smith, Adam, 27–28, 30–31, 35–36, 95
Smollett, Tobias, 47
South Sea Islands, 6–9, 29–30, 71–72

Technology. *See* Commerce and Technology

Totemism, 8, 74–75

Voltaire, 16–17

Watt, Ian, xv–xvi
Wealth, 27–28, 31–32, 36
Whiteness, coding of, 77–78, 88–90
Wordsworth, William: and Carlyle, 43; on childhood, 57; city and country in, xii–xiii; and Conrad, 112; and Dickens, 41; on fetishism and idolatry, 12, 17–18, 20; Hartman on, 16; imagination and fetishism, 14–16, 32, 86, 123; on mansions, 25; on ornament and poetic diction, 20–24, 43; on perception and environment, xii–xiv, 9–10, 41, 46–47, 92, 108, 111–12, 115; on poetry and religion, 19–20, 35; on the sea, 120; whiteness in, 88–90. Works: *Guide to the Lakes*, 25, 88; *Home at Grasmere*, 14; "Intimations of Immortality," 120; "Nutting," 15–16; *The Prelude*, 12, 20, 23–24, 88–90; "A slumber did my spirit seal," 15, 60

The Johns Hopkins University Press

FETISHISM & IMAGINATION

This book was composed in Baskerville text and Bembo display type by Oberlin Printing Company from a design by Lisa S. Mirski. It was printed on S. D. Warren's 50-lb. Sebago Eggshell paper and bound in Kivar 5 by Universal Lithographers.